*Wild Animals
of the World*

Maggie O'Hanlon
Doreen Edmond

*Wild Animals
of the World*

BLANDFORD PRESS
Poole   Dorset

First published in the U.K. 1981 by Blandford Press
Link House, West Street, Poole, Dorset, BH15 1LL
Copyright © 1981 Blandford Books Ltd.

British Library Cataloguing in Publication Data

O'Hanlon, Maggie
  Wild animals of the world. – (New colour series)
  1. Animals
  I. Title   II. Edmond, Doreen   III. Series
  591   QL45.2

ISBN 0 7137 1139 6 (Hardback Edition)
ISBN 0 7137 1145 0 (Paperback Edition)

All rights reserved. No part of this book
may be reproduced or transmitted in any
form or by any means, electronic or
mechanical, including photocopying,
recording or any information storage and
retrieval system, without permission in
writing from the Publisher.

Phototypeset in Monophoto Apollo by
Asco Trade Typesetting Ltd., Hong Kong

Printed in Hong Kong by
South China Printing Co.

Contents

Mammalian orders 6
Introduction 7

1 Polar regions 11
2 Coniferous forests 18
3 Deciduous forest, Mediterranean scrub and evergreen forest 26
4 Grasslands 43
5 Deserts 115
6 Tropical rain forest 122
7 Mountains 146
8 Oceans 154

Bibliography 158
Index of common names 159
Index of Latin names 165

Mammalian orders

PROTOTHERIA (egg-laying mammals)
    MONOTREMATA: duck-billed platypus and echidnas
METATHERIA (pouched mammals)
    MARSUPIALIA: kangaroos, wallabies, phalangers, etc.
EUTHERIA (placental mammals)
    INSECTIVORA: insect-eaters
    CHIROPTERA: bats
    DERMOPTERA: flying lemurs or colugos
    PRIMATES: tree shrews, lemurs, monkeys, apes, man
    EDENTATA: sloths, armadillos, anteaters
    PHOLIDOTA: pangolins
    LAGOMORPHA: pikas, rabbits, hares
    RODENTIA: rodents
    CETACEA: whales, dolphins, porpoises
    CARNIVORA: dogs, weasels, lions, etc.
    PINNIPEDIA: seals, sea-lions, walrus
    TUBULIDENTATA: aardvark
    PROBOSCIDEA: elephants
    HYRACOIDEA: hyraxes
    SIRENIA: manatees, dugong
    PERISSODACTYLA: horses, tapirs, rhinoceroses
    ARTIODACTYLA: pigs, camels, deer, giraffes, antelopes, etc.

Introduction

The term 'animals' is used here in a limited sense to refer to warm, furred creatures belonging to the group known as mammals. This book is intended to introduce the reader, by both picture and description, to a selection of the many and varied mammals of the world, considered in relation to their natural habitats.

WHAT ARE MAMMALS?

The mammals form a major group, or class, of the Animal Kingdom and are distinguished by the possession of a backbone, warm blood and the ability to suckle their young.

In accordance with the principles of Linnaeus, the great Swedish naturalist who laid the foundations of present-day classification, the Mammalia can be divided into three sub-classes: the Prototheria, Metatheria and Eutheria.

The Prototheria is the most primitive group and has only one order, the Monotremata, which is represented by the echidnas (spiny anteaters) and the duck-billed platypus. These are all egg-layers and also show certain other reptilian characteristics. However, when the young hatch, they are suckled by the mother from milk glands which have no teats; the milk exudes from pores in the skin. These pores are the fore-runners of the nipple.

The pouched mammals or Marsupialia, which represent a further stage in mammalian evolution, belong to the Metatheria. The young are born in an immature state and then move to the mother's pouch, which is equipped with teats for suckling, where they remain until their development is complete. This order includes the kangaroos, wallabies, wombats, bandicoots, opossums and pouched mice.

The Eutheria or placental mammals are the most advanced in evolutionary terms. The young are retained within the mother, obtaining oxygen and nourishment *via* the placenta, and are born in an advanced stage of development. The success of this group is reflected in its diversity and in the fact that it contains no less than nineteen orders.

The order Insectivora comprises small primitive creatures, such as hedgehogs, shrews and moles, which feed mainly on insects. The

Chiroptera (bats) are either insect-eaters or fruit-eaters. The sloths, termite-eating anteaters and armadillos make up the order Edentata and are confined to Central and South America, whereas the Pholidota (pangolins), which are similar in many ways to armadillos, but unrelated, come from Africa and Asia. The aardvark, which is also a termite-eater, is quite unique anatomically and is given an order of its own, the Tubulidentata.

Those orders comprised mainly of herbivorous or plant-eating animals include the Lagomorpha, which includes not only the pikas but also the rabbits and hares (which were once classified as rodents) and the Rodentia itself. The Rodentia consists of gnawing animals; it is the largest of all the mammalian orders and includes a great variety of species, ranging from mice, rats, guinea pigs and hamsters to squirrels, beavers and porcupines. In contrast, the Dermoptera, or flying lemurs, contain only two species, both leaf-eaters. The hoofed animals, which are generally referred to as ungulates (from the Latin *unguis* – claw, toe), are also herbivorous. Those with an odd number of toes, the tapirs, rhinoceroses and horses, are known collectively as Perissodactyla. The remainder, the sheep, cattle, deer, antelopes, pigs, giraffes, camels, hippopotami and goats, are all even-toed and known as Artiodactyla. The elephants, both Indian and African, with their distinctive tusks and trunks, belong to the Proboscidea and were at one time thought to be related to the small rock-climbing hyrax. Zoologists have now decided to place the hyrax in an order of its own, the Hyracoidea.

The monkeys, apes, lemurs and man and possibly the tree-shrews, are all Primates and are characterised by their ability to grasp objects with their hands and feet. Their diets are generally mixed.

The numbers of herbivores so far described are relatively great when compared with those of the flesh-eating mammals, the Carnivora, who prey upon them. Generally speaking, all clawed mammals are carnivores and most are very familiar, e.g. the dogs and cats, weasels, badgers, otters and bears.

Some mammals, probably because of competition on land, returned to the sea. There are now three marine orders: the Pinnipedia (seals, sea-lions and walruses), the Sirenia (dugongs and manatees) and the Cetacea (whales, dolphins and porpoises); these show a progressive adaptation to an aquatic existence.

This grouping of animals into orders demonstrates their relationships with each other in a genealogical sense but, more important in terms of survival and understanding the environment, are their relationships with other living things in that environment.

WHAT IS THE ENVIRONMENT?

The environment is the surroundings and conditions which influence the body forms and habits of the animals which it supports and it is characterised most easily by its vegetation.

The predominant vegetation of an area is determined primarily by climate, i.e. temperature, rainfall and day length, although soil and topography also exert an influence. The climate of the world falls into distinct zones, related to latitude but modified by altitude and the proximity of the oceans. This zonation is also seen in the vegetation. Of the ten or so zones recognised by biogeographers, this book describes the following: polar ice, tundra, coniferous, deciduous, evergreen and rain forests, Mediterranean scrub, deserts, grasslands, mountains and oceans.

ADAPTATION TO THE ENVIRONMENT

The survival of any species depends on its ability to adapt to its environment and compete successfully with other species for food and shelter. Adaptations reflect the demands of the environment and may be morphological, e.g. white colouration in the Arctic; physiological, e.g. control of excess water loss in the desert; or behavioural, e.g. burrowing to avoid temperature extremes.

Where the demands of the environment are extremely rigorous, as in the tundra and the desert, only very well adapted animals can survive and the variety of species to be found is small. Conversely, in the rain forest, where there is little temperature fluctuation and abundant food, shelter and water, the greatest variety of species occurs.

In avoiding competition within a particular environment, animals generally become adapted to life in one part of the environment – a 'habitat within a habitat' or *ecological niche*. This is particularly marked in the rain forest. Animals also utilise different food sources.

ADAPTATION AND DIET

Plant-eaters are by far the most numerous and, with the insectivores and smaller carnivores, form the food source of the larger carnivores. The majority of hoofed mammals, particularly those which live in open country, depend on speed, the herding instinct and a colouration which enables them to blend into the background. Horns and antlers are a means of defence. Others, such as the okapi, live deep in the jungle and rely on camouflage. Monkeys and colugos depend on their ability either to climb and leap or to glide. For smaller mammals, retreat into burrows and holes is an important survival factor. Many species, e.g. the prairie marmot and the baboon, have an elaborate social structure which ensures an early warning of danger. Special defence mechanisms are possessed by some species, e.g. the armour-plating of the armadillos and pangolins, the offensive discharge of the skunk and the spines of the hedgehog and porcupine.

The carnivores eat the flesh of weaker or smaller animals. They are all hunters and the lion and tiger are typical examples. Strong, sharp claws, well-developed incisors and stout limb muscles are characteristic of flesh-eaters. They can move quickly over short distances in order to catch their prey and their colouration allows them to blend into the background until the last moment.

There are species, such as the hyena, which, as well as being predators, play an important role as scavengers and feed on the remains of carcasses. Many rodents are omnivorous in habit so that they can take advantage of any available food.

HOW TO USE THIS BOOK

The characteristics of an animal are a result of delicate interplay with its environment and the other occupants in that environment. The mammals in this book have therefore been grouped firstly according to their environment, which is described at the beginning of each section, and secondly according to geography. The geographical divisions are North America, Eurasia (which includes Europe and Asia), the Oriental region (India and the Malaysian archipelago), South America, Africa, and Australasia (Australia, New Zealand and Tasmania). Where an animal is found in more than one country it has been placed in its country of origin or where it is most prevalent.

The descriptions are necessarily brief and are confined mainly to easily recognisable features of form or colour. Each description includes the common name by which the animal is best known. Common names, however, vary from country to country and, to prevent confusion, the scientific name is also given. This is in Latin and, in its simplest form, consists of two words. The first word, which has an initial capital, represents the genus to which the animal belongs. The second word represents the species. A third word sometimes will be found which represents the sub-species. The characters in bold after each description denote the illustration.

1
Polar regions

There are two principal habitats in the polar regions: the ice caps of the Arctic and Antarctic, which consist of permanent ice and snow and are devoid of any vegetation, and the tundra region, which almost encircles the North Pole and extends from the frozen Arctic Ocean to the northern limit of tree growth.

Temperatures on the tundra seldom rise above 10°C in the summer or -18°C in the winter and much of the 25cm annual precipitation falls as snow. The tundra is, in fact, a desert. Summer, which brings the longer days, lasts for only 2–3 months and willows, lichens, mosses, grasses, flowering herbs and berry-bearing bushes appear for this brief growing season.

The number and variety of mammals in these regions is small. The mammals of the ice and snows are all carnivores; the seals, which feed on fish and crustaceans, are the food source of the polar bear. On the tundra, the vegetation, because of its scarcity and limited availability, supports only a limited number of herbivores. Food shortages are overcome in various ways, e.g. migration, hibernation, food storage. The caribou moves southwards during the winter to seek new food supplies but the souslik spends most of the year asleep, emerging only when food is available. Several species make stores of food; the Arctic fox, for example, makes caches of dead lemmings, birds and fish. Other species, such as the musk ox, rely on their reserves of body fat during the winter. A pronounced feature among many tundra mammals is a constant population fluctuation; this phenomenon only serves to emphasise the delicate ecological balance of the habitat.

Apart from food, heat conservation is the other main problem for polar mammals. To prevent heat loss, their bodies are generally large, so that the total body surface is small in relation to bulk. Tails and ears tend to be small for the same reason. Insulation is provided either by thick layers of fat or blubber, as in the seals and walruses, or by thick fur, as in the musk ox and polar bear. The coat is generally made up of a double layer of hairs: the long outer ones are oily and waterproof while the inner ones are denser and form pockets which trap air. The coat becomes thicker in winter. Feet and ears also tend to be furry to conserve heat.

For concealment, and possibly to prevent heat loss, many animals have white coats. Some, such as the polar bear, are white all the year round. The stoat and the varying hare, however, are white in the winter and coloured in the summer.

A few species, including the caribou and polar bear, have especially large feet which spread their weight and prevent the animals from sinking into the snow or breaking the ice on which they move. Hairs on the soles provide extra grip as well as insulation.

Those animals which are not fully adapted, morphologically or physiologically, to withstand the severe conditions, often show behavioural adaptations. Deep burrows, such as those of the souslik, are a good way of avoiding extremes of temperature. Another common feature is a fast maturation rate. The majority of tundra mammals give birth in the spring but, by the end of the brief summer, the offspring are sufficiently developed to face the hazards of the winter.

ARCTIC ICE

Ring seal   *Pusa hispida*   PINNIPEDIA
This species occurs mainly in the Arctic Ocean, with a few scattered populations in the Baltic and the Gulfs of Bothnia and Finland.

The coarse coat is grey-black to brownish black on the back and bears conspicuous straw-coloured rings. The sides and belly are whitish yellow. The body is 102–183cm long with a tail of a further 10cm. The seal weighs from 36–110kg.

It lives on or under the ice in winter and on banks or reefs in the summer. It feeds on fish and crustaceans. A single pup is born in March–April and mating occurs about 1 month afterwards. **1a**

Polar bear   *Thalarctos maritimus*   CARNIVORA
This bear has a circumpolar range, from Siberia to Spitsbergen, Greenland, Labrador and northern Canada.

It is one of the largest species of bear; a fully grown male may be up to 275cm long, including the small tail of 7.5–10cm, and up to 153cm high at the shoulder. The average weight is 408kg, although weights up to 725kg have been recorded. The head is longer and narrower than in most bears, the ears small and rounded, the neck long and the limbs stout. The feet have hairy soles to grip the ice and the toes are webbed for swimming. The fur, which is white or yellowish white, enables the animal to blend into the background of snowy wastes in which it lives.

A very good swimmer, the polar bear feeds mainly on seals. The cubs, normally twins, are born during December. **1b**

Atlantic walrus   *Odobenus rosmarus rosmarus*   PINNIPEDIA
This walrus ranges from Siberia through Greenland as far west as Hudson's Bay in Canada. It name is derived from the Scandinavian *valross* meaning 'whale-horse'.

It resembles the sea-lions in having hind flippers which can be turned forward but has no external ears and the canine teeth protrude downwards from the upper jaw to form parallel tusks. The head, which is small compared with the body, has long coarse whiskers on the upper lip. The skin is covered with brownish hair at first but becomes almost naked with increasing age and is much folded and wrinkled. Fully grown males are up to 365cm long and weigh up to 1360kg.

The walrus feeds on crabs, shellfish and sea-urchins, which it collects from the sea floor. It comes ashore to breed and a single calf is born in May. **1c**

Harp seal   *Pagophilus groenlandicus*   PINNIPEDIA
The harp or Greenland seal is an Arctic species, ranging from the Kara Sea around Novya Zemlya, through Spitsbergen, Jan Mayen and Greenland to north-eastern Canada.

It is 155–218cm long and weighs 117–179kg. The male is yellowish white or greyish yellow in colour with a brownish black area running from the shoulders to the sides of the tail. Most of the head is dark. The female is greyer and smaller.

Fish and crustaceans, caught at depths of 180m or more, comprise the diet. Breeding occurs in the spring, in dense colonies on the drift ice, and there are 1–2 pups in a litter. **1d**

ANTARCTIC ICE

Ross seal   *Ommatophoca rossi*   PINNIPEDIA
This solitary seal lives on the pack ice around the southern polar land-mass.

The body is large and thickset and up to 230cm long. The head is short with a thick neck region, large chubby cheeks and large eyes. The dark grey colour of the back grades into a pale under side.

It is thought to eat mainly squid and octopus, although fish are also taken. Little is known of its breeding habits. **2a**

Weddell seal   *Leptonychotes weddelli*   PINNIPEDIA
The Weddell seal is found in the Southern Ocean, particularly in the

Weddell Sea, and lives in colonies close to land.

It grows up to 305cm long. The female, which is the larger, weighs up to 476kg. The back is black and the ever-increasing white lines and patches along the sides grade into the pale grey or white belly.

It spends most of the winter in the water, breathing by means of holes which it makes in the ice. The pups are born in September–October and are weaned at about 2 months. They feed on crustaceans before changing to the adult diet of fish. **2b**

Crabeater seal   *Lobodon carcinophagus*   PINNIPEDIA
The crabeater is found throughout the Southern Ocean between the polar coast and the pack ice. It moves north in the winter and occasionally may be found in Australian, New Zealand and South American waters.

It grows up to 275cm long and weighs up to 249kg. The body is dark grey with a brown tint on the back, shading to a pale, almost white, colour on the under side. The sides are marked with a variable pattern of brown rings. In summer, the colour fades to almost white.

The crabeater feeds exclusively on shrimp-like crustaceans known as krill. The jaws and teeth are adapted to act as a sieve. Little is known of its breeding habits. **2c**

Southern elephant seal   *Mirounga leonina*   PINNIPEDIA
The elephant seal is found mostly in the southern oceans, breeding on islands such as South Georgia, Heard and Kerguelen. Hunting has greatly reduced its numbers.

This gigantic seal can weigh up to 2268kg. A fully grown male may reach 549cm in length and has a characteristic proboscis, or trunk, which usually hangs limply from the muzzle but can be inflated to 60–90cm. The female is rarely more than 305cm long and has no proboscis. The skin is usually greyish, often tinged with olive, and is darker on the upper parts.

The diet consists mainly of squid. From February–June, the females give birth to 1–2 calves, 75cm long when born. They are weaned at 6 weeks. **2d**

NORTH AMERICAN TUNDRA

Arctic souslik   *Citellus undulatus*   RODENTIA
The Arctic souslik or ground squirrel is found throughout the tundra zone and is remarkable in being the only tundra mammal to hibernate.

It is a fairly large rodent (up to 700g). The back is brownish with paler spots and under parts. The ears are small. Although the large body size prevents excessive heat loss, nevertheless the souslik spends 9 months of the year in hibernation. It builds a deep burrow, leading to a chamber lined with grasses for insulation; it usually lives as part of a community.

It emerges in April–May, to feed on shoots, seeds and some animal food and to rear its 6–9 young. In August–September it returns to hibernation. **3a**

Caribou *Rangifer tarandus caribou* ARTIODACTYLA
The caribou of North America and the reindeer of northern Europe are slightly different forms of the same species.

Among deer, both animals are remarkable as both males and females carry antlers. These arise from the upper part of the skull; in the bulls, the brow tines are fully developed and descend over the face; in the reindeer the lower tines are more branched and shorter. The male caribou is about 107cm high at the shoulder, 1.9m long and weighs up to 181kg. The female is lighter (125kg). The hooves are broad and flat and deeply cleft for walking in deep snow.

Grasses, leaves and, especially in winter, lichens form the diet. The bulls form 'harems' of 30–40 cows in September–October. The 1–2 calves can walk within a few hours of birth and are weaned at 2 months. **3b**

Musk ox *Ovibos moschatus* ARTIODACTYLA
The musk ox lives in herds in north Canada and Greenland and is so-called because of the musk glands on the face of the bull.

It is large and heavily built, up to 152cm high at the shoulder. The dense, dark brown, long-haired coat, which reaches the ground in winter, makes it appear even larger. The head is large with a hairy muzzle. The horns, which are broad and flattened at the base, almost meet in the centre and curve downwards and outwards before rising at the tips. The ears are small and almost invisible under the hair.

It browses on the available vegetation. The single calf is born in May, weighing about 6kg, and can follow the cow after 1 hour. **3c**

Wolf *Canis lupus* CARNIVORA
The wolf is one of the largest of the wild dogs. It is found in western North America, Florida and Mexico and still occurs in remote parts of Spain, France, Germany, Scandinavia and northern Asia.

Strongly built with strong jaws and teeth and long, powerful legs, an adult male is about 137cm long with a 41cm tail and stands about 79cm at the shoulder. The fur is whitish grey to yellow-grey according to race. In the Arctic, it may be white.

The wolf lives alone or in pairs, forming packs only when food is scarce. It hunts for smaller mammals and birds by day and lies up at night in its den. Mating occurs in January–March and a litter of 5–9 cubs is produced after 60–63 days. **3d**

EURASIAN TUNDRA

Stoat   *Mustela erminea erminea*   CARNIVORA
The stoat or ermine distributed widely through Europe, parts of Asia eastwards to Japan, and in north Africa. It is also found in North America, where it is known as the short-tailed weasel.

The male is 28–33cm long overall, the female slightly smaller. The body is long and lithe with short legs. The head is broad, with small rounded ears, and the tail is 10–13cm long. The coat is pure white in winter, except for the black bushy tip of the tail (the form known as ermine), but changes to reddish brown with yellowish under parts after the spring moult.

Birds, eggs and small mammals form the main diet but fish and aquatic animals may also be taken. The young are born in April–May, 4–5 in a litter, and blind and naked. **4a**

Arctic fox   *Alopex lagopus*   CARNIVORA
The Arctic fox is found from Scandinavia to eastern Siberia, Alaska, Arctic Canada and Greenland.

A small species, seldom longer than 60cm, it differs from other foxes in several ways. The muzzle is blunter and shorter, the ears are smaller and rounded and the cheeks are fringed with long hair—all adaptations to prevent heat loss. The fur is typically white for camouflage but some foxes also undergo a bluish colour phase and are much sought after by fur traders. As in the polar bear, the feet have hairy soles to grip the ice and snow.

The Arctic fox feeds on birds, stranded fish and lemmings. It does not hibernate, but stores dead lemmings in rock crevices for the winter, supplementing its diet from the remains of prey of the polar bear. The cubs, 6–8 in number, are born in the spring. **4b**

Norwegian lemming *Lemmus lemmus* RODENTIA

This small burrowing rodent is commonly found in colonies in the Scandinavian mountains but also occurs further south in hilly districts.

The body is about 13cm long overall with a short stumpy tail, thick fur and tiny ears. The colour is unusually bright for a rodent: black and rusty yellow on the upper parts and rusty yellow beneath.

Periodically, possibly because of population pressure, lemmings migrate *en masse* from their homes and those reaching the sea drown. Grasses, roots and lichens are the staple diet. Lemmings do not hibernate and the female gives birth to 5–6 young. **4c**

Varying hare *Lepus timidus* LAGOMORPHA

The varying, Arctic or blue hare is found in Iceland and Faeroes, throughout Scandinavia and eastwards through the USSR to the Pacific.

It is 46–61cm long with a short tail of 3–7.5cm. The coat is white or greyish in the winter, although the ear tips stay black, and brownish in the summer. The ears are relatively short which reduces heat loss. An adult weighs between 2 and 6kg.

This hare is generally active at night. It feeds on green plants in the summer and the shoots and bark of woody plants, and lichens, in the winter. 1–3 litters are produced in a season. The number of young varies between 1 and 8. **4d**

2
Coniferous forest

The coniferous forest, also known as the *taiga* or *boreal forest*, extends in a belt around the Northern Hemisphere, between the tundra and latitude 50°N. It also occurs at high altitudes elsewhere.

The climate which supports this vegetation is characterised by a temperature range of $-30°C$ to $20°C$ and an annual precipitation of between 30cm and 74cm. Snow is present for most of the year and rainfall occurs mainly during the 3–5 months of summer.

The soil, known as *podsol*, is poor and acid and lacks nutrients. Often a layer of iron develops, called *hardpan*, which tree roots cannot penetrate and which prevents drainage.

Nevertheless, vegetation abounds in the form of coniferous trees: white spruce, balsam firs, redwoods and jack pines in North America and Norway spruce, Scotch pines, larches and firs in Eurasia. Deciduous trees, e.g. birch and aspen, also occur in scattered pockets and in increasing numbers where the coniferous forest merges with the deciduous forest of lower latitudes. The conifers owe their success to the following adaptations: shallow roots, a concentrated sap which does not freeze at low temperatures and a conical shape which allows the snow to fall off easily so that the branches do not get broken by the weight.

To the mammals of the coniferous forest, snow is probably the most significant problem. It may be several yards deep, presenting a difficult surface over which to move and covering the herbage and undergrowth which forms the diet of many species.

Various ways of overcoming the problem of locomotion are to be encountered. The moose, which moves *through* the snow, has very long legs and a 'straight up and down' gait, so that its hooves are not dragged through the snow. The lynx has large furry feet which act as 'snowshoes', spreading the animal's weight. Many species have resorted to the trees, e.g. martens and squirrels, and the flying squirrel has become further adapted to glide from tree to tree. The porcupine is particularly versatile and is equally at home moving over land, climbing trees or, by virtue of its hollow quills, swimming. Small rodents move *beneath* the snow cover. Because of the heat radiated by the ground, a space is formed between the ground and the snow by a process called *sublimation*. Temperature in this space is constant and always a few degrees higher than that at the surface. It is here that the small rodents, such as the shrews, are found and also carnivores, such as the slinky-bodied weasels, that prey on them.

Winter food shortages are dealt with in various ways. Snow not only covers up suitable food plants but also raises the ground level in relation to the trees and weighs down the branches, bringing them within reach of the larger herbivores. It is, therefore not surprising to find that some deer change their diet accordingly in winter. Considerable weight loss may be experienced by many animals but this is made up in the spring.

Flexibility of diet is fairly common, particularly among the bears. Squirrels and chipmunks hoard food for the winter and some species, e.g. the black bear, squirrel and chipmunk go into a deep sleep (not true hibernation) when conditions are extreme.

The snowshoe rabbit is probably the most remarkable species in this habitat as regards colouration, being white in the winter and brown in the summer. Formation of brown pigment is related to daylength. It also experiences the extreme population fluctuations which are found in so many species of mammals from the tundra.

NORTH AMERICA

North American flying squirrel   *Glaucomys volans*   RODENTIA
A close relation of the true squirrel, the flying squirrel lives in woodland areas of the southern parts of Canada and Alaska and southwards into the eastern and central USA as far as Texas.

The squirrel is distinguished by the skin membrane, which extends along the flanks and unites the fore and hind limbs. This acts as a parachute, which enables it to glide from tree to tree in a downward slanting direction. The fur is brownish above and whitish below. As in most nocturnal animals, the eyes are large. The ears are comparatively small without ear tufts.

The squirrel feeds at night, mainly on nuts, fruits, seeds and insects. It spends the day in hollow trees or sometimes buildings. Mating occurs in February–March. A litter of 2–6 young is produced after 40 days' gestation. **5a**

Grizzly bear   *Ursus arctos horribilis*   CARNIVORA
The grizzly bear is so closely related to the brown bear of Eurasia that it is generally thought to be the same species. Its original range, throughout the mountains of western America from Mexico to the Arctic, is now restricted to the Rocky Mountains between Oregon and Alaska.

The largest American carnivore, a fully grown male grizzly is up to 260cm long, 91–122cm high and weighs up to 360kg. The fur is generally brown, varying from yellowish to greyish, with many white-tipped hairs on the back. The ears are small and rounded, the muzzle and snout pointed and the tail very small. The legs are stout and powerful; the feet have 5 toes with retractile claws.

It feeds on small- and medium-sized birds and mammals and also takes fish. Large amounts of roots, berries and fruits are also eaten. It lives alone or in a family group with usually 2–4 cubs. **5b**

Canada lynx   *Felis lynx canadensis*   CARNIVORA
This lynx and the Eurasian lynx are generally considered to be races of the same species. As its name suggests, its range is restricted to Canada.

It is a medium-sized cat about 90cm long, including a short, black-tipped tail of 13cm. The legs are very strong, to enable it to spring onto its prey, and the broad furry feet stop it from sinking into the snow. The yellowish brown coat is slightly spotted, with paler under parts. The ears have distinctive black tufts and there are also two black tassels on the throat.

The lynx feeds on small rodents, birds, small deer and the occasional moose or reindeer. The young are born in the summer after 60 days' gestation. **5c**

Marmot   *Marmota monax*   RODENTIA
The marmot or woodchuck lives in the mountainous areas of Canada and the USA, between the tree-line and the snow-line.

Like the closely related alpine marmot, it is stockily built, with short limbs and small ears. The relatively long tail balances the animal when it sits upright on its hind legs to feed or to see better. The fur is a grizzled reddish brown, darker on the head, back and tail.

The marmot is diurnal and feeds on a great variety of vegetation during the summer months, building up reserves of fat for hibernation. It is a sociable creature, living in colonies in extensive burrow systems. **5d**

Eastern chipmunk   *Tamias striatus*   RODENTIA

Chipmunks can be distinguished from their close relations, the true squirrels, by the presence of cheek pouches for the storage of food. This particular chipmunk lives in the eastern USA, among tall grasses and scattered bushes, often in areas of rock and fallen timber.

It is about 18cm long, with a tail of another 10cm, and weighs about 140g. The back is greyish, marked with 5 heavy black stripes which extend from the shoulders to the root of the tail. The under parts are fawn and there are white stripes above and below the eyes. The small ears are not tufted.

The chipmunk is gregarious and digs extensive burrows up to 1m deep. It feeds on nuts, berries, seeds and grain. After mating in February–March, and a gestation of 35 days, the female produces 3–5 young. **5e**

American marten   *Martes americana*   CARNIVORA

The marten is found throughout the coniferous forests of Canada, southwards into the western USA.

It is about 90cm long overall and weighs 0.9–1.4kg. The body is extremely supple and covered in luxurious brown fur which is highly prized in the trade. The toes are long and flexible, with strong claws for climbing. The tail, which is very bushy, helps in balancing.

The marten is generally active by day, feeding mainly on red squirrels, but also on partridges, rabbits, chipmunks and carrion. It is solitary except when breeding. 3–4 young are born in the spring. **5f**

Least weasel   *Mustela nivalis rixosa*   CARNIVORA

The American and Eurasian weasels are races of the same species.

A fully grown male is 28cm long, including a tail of 6.5cm, and weighs about 225g. The female is slightly smaller. The coat is reddish brown above and white on the under parts. The body is long and sinuous with short legs. There are well developed scent glands.

The diet consists of small rodents, rabbits, birds, insects, reptiles and frogs. The weasel nests in a hole and here the 4–6 young are born after a gestation of 35 days. **6a**

Black bear   *Ursus americanus*   CARNIVORA

The black bear, which is the most numerous of the bears in North America, is common throughout the forested areas of Canada and the northern USA.

It is heavy-bodied with a broad head, narrow jaws, short legs and a stumpy tail. It is smaller than the brown bear, an adult male weighs about 136kg, and more rounded in shape. The colour of the coat ranges through all shades of brown to black. This bear is also a very good climber.

Although technically a carnivore it supplements its diet of small mammals with grasses, bulbs, berries and bees' and wasps' nests. In the north of its range, it falls into a deep sleep during the winter (not true hibernation) in caves or holes. Mating occurs every 2 years and the cubs, usually 2, are born in the winter den. **6b**

Canadian porcupine   *Erethizon dorsatum*   RODENTIA
This porcupine is widespread in the forests of Canada and the western USA.

It is about 60cm long, with a tail of 923cm, and it weighs 4.5–7kg when fully grown. The quills are shorter than those of Old World porcupines and are hidden in winter by the long silky hair which grows between them. They are used for defence. The feet are modified for tree-climbing: the sole is wide, a broad movable pad on the hind foot replaces the first toe, and the claws are strong and curved.

Leaves and buds are the staple diet in summer and bark from the upper branches in winter. The porcupine is solitary and nocturnal and does not hibernate. A single young is born after 7 months' gestation. **6c**

Moose   *Alces alces*   ARTIODACTYLA
The moose, the largest deer, is closely related to the elk of Europe. It lives in well-watered forest areas of Canada, the northern USA and Alaska, near to water in summer and in higher forest areas in winter.

An adult male stands up to 236cm at the shoulder and weighs up to 363kg. The fur is long and coarse, generally darkish brown with paler legs. The female is usually paler. There is a slight mane on the neck and shoulders and longer hair on the throat. The antlers span up to 198cm, and have a short tineless beam, expanding into a flattened area with many tines. The head is long and narrow, with large ears. The neck is short.

The moose feeds mainly on leaves and tree bark. It is polygamous. Mating occurs in the autumn and 1–3 calves are born 8–9 months later. **6d**

Snowshoe rabbit   *Lepus americanus*   LAGOMORPHA
The snowshoe rabbit, also known as the snowshoe or varying hare, is, in fact, a true hare and is found in the coniferous forests of Canada

and the northern USA.

It has a more compact body and rather shorter ears than the hares of more temperate climates. In the autumn and winter months the coat is white, although the ears have blackish tips, but in spring and summer the coat becomes brown speckled with black hairs. The under side is paler. Stiff bristles on the feet provide insulation and ease of movement across the snow and ice.

This hare is mainly active at night except in very hard weather. Its winter diet consists of shoots, bark, woody plants and lichens but it takes advantage of fresh greenery in the summer. **6e**

Canadian beaver   *Castor canadiensis*   RODENTIA
This heavily built aquatic rodent occurs in Canada and some northern districts of the USA.

It is about 76cm long, with a broad, flat, scaly tail up to 30cm long, and weighs up to 27kg. The hind feet are strongly webbed and the fore feet have sharp claws for digging. The large, rounded head has small ears which, like the nostrils, can be closed under water. The thick soft fur is dark brown and the legs are short and stout. With its sharp front teeth, it fells small trees which it uses to dam streams, thus forming small lakes. Here it lives, in colonies, in 'lodges' constructed of timber and mud.

It feeds on the bark of trees. Mating occurs in January–February and 1–8 young are born 2–4 months later. **6f**

EURASIA

Red squirrel   *Sciurus vulgaris*   RODENTIA
This species is typically European, with several local races which extend across much of Asia. It was formerly common in the British Isles but has been replaced in many areas by the larger more aggressive grey squirrel.

The red squirrel is about 23cm long with a bushy tail of another 18cm. It has larger ears than its grey cousin, with tufts at the tips in winter, when the coat is brownish red. In the British Isles, the coat becomes shorter in summer, the ear tufts disappear and the tail bleaches to a yellowish white. In Scandinavia, the tail remains red and the winter coat is more greyish brown.

Nuts, acorns, fruit and plant buds are the staple diet. The red squirrel builds its drey in tall trees and gives birth to 2–4 young, usually in May. **7a**

Pine marten   *Martes martes*   CARNIVORA

The pine marten is found over much of Europe, including the British Isles, and belongs to the mustelid (weasel) family. The bushy tail accounts for 15–23cm of the pine marten's 70–76cm overall length. The muzzle is pointed and the ears are large and pointed. The toes are furnished with long, curved claws which enable it to climb trees. The long supple body is a rich dark brown, marked only by a yellow area on the throat.

It is nocturnal and arboreal in habit and feeds on small mammals, especially squirrels, voles, rats, mice and birds. The gestation period is 8–9 weeks and there are 4–6 young in a litter. **7b**

Wolverine   *Gulo gulo*   CARNIVORA

The wolverine or glutton is a powerfully built member of the weasel family and ranges from the Arctic and sub-Arctic parts of Eurasia to North America.

It is about 122cm long, including the 30cm long tail, stands about 35cm at the shoulder and weighs up to 16kg. The head is round and broad with a short, pointed muzzle, small eyes set wide apart and very small rounded ears. The body appears rather clumsy with the arched back and stumpy, bushy tail. The long coarse fur is darkish brown on the back, yellow-brown on the flanks, with dark brown under parts.

The wolverine will eat almost anything, from deer and cattle to lemmings, hares and fish, and is renowned for its destructiveness, strength and appetite. Mating occurs in February–April and, after 2–4 months, 2–3 young are born in a den in a hollow tree. **7c**

Brown bear   *Ursus arctos*   CARNIVORA

Formerly common throughout Eurasia, this bear is now found only in USSR, northern Scandinavia and the Balkans. It is related to the grizzly bear of North America.

It is characterised by its colour and the large wide head and short muzzle. The neck is short and thick, the ears small and rounded and the limbs stout. The tail is vestigial. The coat is thick and long in winter with a soft woolly under fur and is brown or greyish brown, according to season and locality. The brown bear hibernates in the colder parts of its range.

Fish, berries, honey and grubs form the major part of the diet, with occasional mammals and birds. The young, usually 2, are born during the winter. The cubs are about 20cm long at birth and weigh 0.7kg but reach up to 27kg after a year. **7d**

Common European shrew   *Sorex araneus*   INSECTIVORA
The common shrew is found in all parts of the British Isles, except Ireland, and in much of central Europe and parts of Asia. It lives in long grass and undergrowth.

Superficially, it resembles a mouse but it is easily distinguished by the long, pointed snout, which extends beyond the lower lip, and by the flattened, rounded ears. The eyes are small and beady. There is a musk gland on each flank and the smell emitted affords a certain amount of protection from enemies such as owls.

Shrews feed on insects and worms. Several litters of 5–8 young are born during the summer. **7e**

Weasel   *Mustela nivalis nivalis*   CARNIVORA
The weasel ranges across practically the whole of Eurasia to Japan and is also found in northern Africa.

The male is about 20cm long with a tail of a further 6–7.5cm. The female is considerably smaller. The body is long and slender. The head and muzzle are sharply pointed and the legs are short. The ears are small. The coat is reddish brown above and white below and the tail, unlike that of the stoat, has no black tip.

Weasels prey on small mammals – rabbits, rats, voles and mice, and also small birds. They sometimes go into the water for water voles and frogs. The weasel generally has 2 litters a year, each of 4–6 young. They are born in a nest lined with grasses and dried leaves. The gestation period is 35 days. **7f**

3
Deciduous forest, Mediterranean scrub and evergreen forest

Deciduous forest is composed of trees that lose all their leaves for part of the year. In temperate and monsoon regions, leaf fall is governed by seasonal effects of temperature, day-length and rainfall. In subtropical regions and the higher-lying areas of the tropical regions, there is little or no seasonal effect and the forest is 'evergreen' because the trees are all at different stages, some losing their leaves, others coming into bud and others in full leaf. True evergreens, i.e. trees that never lose all their leaves at once, are particularly characteristic of the Mediterranean.

The largest tracts of deciduous forest occur in the Northern Hemisphere, in North America, Europe and north-east China, but there are also areas on the west coast of southern South America and parts of Australia. The average rainfall is 75–155cm and it is distributed fairly evenly throughout the year. The temperature does not fall below 0°C for any great length of time and there are four well-defined seasons. The soil, known as *mull* or *brown earth*, is particularly fertile because of the large amount of humus derived from the falling leaves. The trees themselves are broadleaved to absorb the maximum amount of light and include hickory, oak, birch, beech, maple, hazel and chestnut. In the autumn, when the temperatures start to fall and the days become shorter, the trees lose their leaves. This enables them to withstand the winter drought, when low temperatures reduce the amount of available water. Growth is resumed in the spring and, by summer, the trees are in full leaf. The leaves form the *canopy* layer and, in this type of forest, the canopy is sufficiently open to allow the sunlight to penetrate. The forest floor, therefore, supports a rich plant growth – the *herb layer* – particularly in spring when the leaf cover is at its lightest. Above this, to a height of about 6m, are the bushes and shrubs.

In the warm temperate zones, the summers are hotter (over 20°C) and drier and the winters are warm and wet. Rainfall decreases to between 25cm and 75cm a year and the soil is generally poor. The vegetation, termed Mediterranean scrub, although it is by no means confined to the Mediterranean, is adapted to withstand drought and most plants are *sclerophytic*, i.e. they have a hard cuticle on the leaves to prevent water loss. The trees, olive, citrus, cork oak, cypress, are evergreen and low and branching in appearance. They tend to be scattered. Ground cover is sparse and many plants have bulbous tap roots for conserving water. Oils and resins, present in plants such as thyme, oregano and juniper, also help to prevent dessication. Such vegetation is known by various names in the countries in which it occurs: as *mallee* in Australia, *maquis* or *garigue* in the Mediterranean areas, *chaparral* in California, USA. Similar areas are also found in central Chile and North Island, New Zealand.

The areas of monsoon forest, which extend through peninsular India, eastern Java and the Lesser Sunda Islands, experience summer temperatures of over 25°C and an annual rainfall of up to 200cm. However, the rainfall is confined almost entirely to the hot wet season and during the hot dry and cool dry seasons there are drought conditions. The vegetation consists largely of *sal* trees and the open nature of the forest allows the growth of shrubs and bushes.

Where the temperatures are less extreme and the rainfall is more evenly distributed, broadleaved evergreen forest, consisting of species such as beech, oak, teak, camphor, bamboo and, in Australia, eucalyptus, is found. The coastal areas of the southern half of Australia, the eastern lowlands and the western mountains of southern China, the Himalayas and the central areas of the Americas support such vegetation. The density of the forest varies with rainfall; on the drier mountain slopes there is less undergrowth.

The many levels of these forests offer a great range of habitats. On the forest floor, where there are a great number of insects, grasses, roots, bulbs, fallen nuts and fruits, there are the insectivorous shrew and numbat, omnivores, such as the hedgehog, badger and rat, and herbivores, such as the wild boar and wombat. The undergrowth, which is more abundant than that of the rain forest supports a relatively greater population of browsing and grazing animals. These tend to be larger than the browsers of the rain forest and they can build up food reserves in the body to withstand shortages in the dormant or drought periods. The smaller species, e.g. the rabbit, feed on the lower levels of the shrubs and bushes. The deer and tahr feed on the upper levels and the largest species, e.g. the wapiti, feed on the leaves of young trees.

There are fewer fully arboreal species than in the rain forest because of the lack of cover, and food sources, during the dormant periods. Some northern species, such as the squirrel, dormouse and bats, sleep or hibernate at this time. Most arboreal creatures are found in the evergreen forests, e.g. koala and gliders, and it is mainly here that flying and gliding have evolved as a means of getting from tree to tree. The majority of carnivores are found at ground level e.g. dingo, thylacine, red fox, but some, such as the raccoon and North American opossum, are well adapted for climbing and can range widely in their search for food. Aquatic animals such as the otter and the platypus live in the rivers in clearings in the forest.

DECIDUOUS FOREST: NORTH AMERICA

Common opossum *Didelphis marsupialis* MARSUPIALIA
The common or Virginian opossum is found in many parts of the USA, extending westwards to southern California and south to Mexico. It lives in trees or bushes, in burrows or hollow tree trunks.

About the size of a cat, it has a long, naked, prehensile tail, which is used in climbing trees. The head is pointed, with rat-like ears, and the limbs are more or less equal in length. There is a coarse outer coat of bristly greyish to white fur and the legs are black.

The opossum is nocturnal and feeds on small birds and animals, fruit, roots, eggs and carrion. In the south, this species usually has 2 litters a year, in the north only 1. The gestation period is 8–13 days and there are about 18 young in each litter. These remain in the mother's pouch for about 10 weeks, after which they are carried on her back. **8a**

Grey squirrel *Sciurus carolinensis* RODENTIA
Originally from Carolina, this species extends throughout North America and, since its introduction in the 19th century, throughout England as well.

The grey squirrel is 20–25cm long with a tail of almost equal length. It is pale to medium grey above and whitish below. Its ears are small and rounded with no ear tufts.

It prefers mixed woodland where it builds large dreys of twigs and leaves, or sometimes a nest in a hollow tree. It feeds by day on nuts, berries, beech mast, birds' eggs and sometimes carrion. It also eats the bark and buds of trees, causing considerable damage to plantations.

Mating occurs in January–August. The gestation period is 30–44 days and there are 1–6 young in a litter. They leave the nest after about 6 weeks. **8b**

Wapiti   *Cervus canadensis*   ARTIODACTYLA
The wapiti is found in the more westerly states of North America, from Canada south to the Yellowstone Park, in forested mountain regions.

It is closely related to the European red deer. A fully grown male is about 158cm high at the shoulder, with antlers about 152cm long. These are very smooth, with backward curves and 5–7 points each. Stags weigh about 340kg, hinds about 227kg. The adult is greyish brown, with dark chestnut on the upper parts and a grey patch on the rump. The calves are much paler, almost yellow-brown with white spots.

The diet consists of grasses and the leaves and shoots of deciduous trees. The hinds produce 1–3 calves weighing about 14kg each at birth. Wapiti become sexually mature at 3 years and may live for 22 years. **8c**

White-tailed deer   *Odocoileus virginianus*   ARTIODACTYLA
One of the best known and most graceful of American deer, this species ranges from southern Canada throughout the USA, with related forms in Central and South America.

A fully grown male is just over 90cm high at the shoulder. In summer, the coat is reddish brown above and white below, becoming greyish brown in the winter. The throat, muzzle ring, eye spots, insides of the ears and the long tail are also white. The antlers, which are only found in the male, are fairly short, with 5–6 points. A browser, the animal feeds on twigs, buds, fruits and fresh ground vegetation.

The fawns, usually 2 or 3 at birth, are reddish brown, spotted with white for the first 4 months. **8d**

Bay lynx   *Felis rufa*   CARNIVORA
This species, also known as the bobcat, is smaller than the Canada lynx and ranges through much of the wooded country in the southern USA, where it makes lairs in hollows and caves or, occasionally, in hollow trees.

About 60–76cm long, the fur is a rusty yellow-brown generally with large dark spots on the body and dark stripes on the face. There is also a dark stripe down the centre of the back. The throat, which has a ruff of long hair, and the under parts are white, the latter spotted with darker markings. The ears are typically tufted whilst the tail is short and stumpy.

The bay lynx emerges at dusk or dawn to hunt for small mammals and the smaller game birds, such as grouse and partridge. It lives alone or in a family group of 2 parents and their young. 2–3 cubs are born at a time, after 40 days' gestation. **8e**

North American raccoon   *Procyon lotor*   CARNIVORA
The raccoon ranges over much of North and Central America, as far south as Costa Rica. It is widely hunted for its fur.

The body is stoutly built, just under 60cm long, and the bushy tail, which is about 25cm long, has characteristic alternate black and brown rings. It weighs 7–11kg. The head is broad with a sharp muzzle and the ears are small and rounded. The fur, which is thick and coarse, is a mixture of black, grey and brown. The lower part of the face is white with a black mask around the eyes. The limbs are short and powerful and the feet strongly clawed for climbing trees.

The raccoon is nocturnal, emerging at dusk to hunt for mice, birds' eggs, small birds, frogs, fish, crayfish and even cereals. The gestation period is 63–70 days and there are 3–6 young in a litter. **8f**

Striped skunk   *Mephitis mephitis*   CARNIVORA
This cat-sized mammal, with long glossy black fur marked with white on the forehead and down the middle of the flanks, is found in all but the northernmost parts of North America. It lives in burrows on the forest edges.

The long bushy tail is usually black with white towards the tip, and is curled over the back when moving. The pattern of the white markings varies according to race. The head is small with a pointed muzzle, the ears are small and rounded, and the compact elongated body has short legs, with long feet, straight toes and blunt, curved claws. Skunks are renowned for the evil-smelling liquid which they can eject from their anal glands for distances up to 3.5m.

They are nocturnal, feeding on insects, snakes, frogs, birds' eggs or small mammals. There are 4–10 young in a litter. **8g**

DECIDUOUS FOREST: EURASIA

Hazel dormouse   *Muscardinus avellanarius*   RODENTIA
The dormouse is found all over Europe, including the British Isles and extending into Asia Minor. It lives in woods, thickets and copses,

frequently of hazel.

About the size of a small mouse, it has a large head and ears and particularly large black eyes. The tail is long, furry, and cylindrical. The young are usually mouse-grey but the adult is light yellowish red above and paler yellow below, sometimes with a whitish patch on the throat and upper chest.

It is nocturnal and feeds on nuts, insects, eggs and nestlings. From September to April, it hibernates in a nest of twigs and grasses. There are usually several litters a year, from May onwards, each of 3–4 young. The gestation period is 21 days. **9a**

Wild boar   *Sus scrofa*   ARTIODACTYLA

The wild boar occurs in forest and swampy country in many parts of Europe, eastwards to central Asia.

A fully grown male is about 90cm high at the shoulder and 122cm long. The elongated head has a truncated snout, flattened and naked at the tip. The slender legs end in small hooves, each with 4 well developed toes. The coat of bristly hairs is pale grey to blackish brown with a woolly under fur. The young are brownish grey with light yellowish stripes on the under side of the body. The canine teeth, or tushes, are elongated. The upper pair turn upwards and rub on the inner surface of the lower pair.

The wild boar eats almost anything. 3–12 piglets are born after a gestation period of 112–115 days. **9b**

Red deer   *Cervus elaphus*   ARTIODACTYLA

The red deer is found over most of Europe, from southern Scandinavia to the southern Balkans, and also in the British Isles, particularly Scotland.

A fully grown stag is about 122cm high at the shoulder with antlers up to 109cm long, each bearing up to 6 tines. The antlers are shed every March. The females, or hinds, are smaller and lack antlers. The coat is reddish brown in summer, more grey in winter. There is a considerable throat fringe. The tail is quite short and surrounded by a buff patch.

The red deer lives in herds, headed by an old, experienced stag and feeds on grass and vegetation. Rutting occurs in November. The single, dappled calf is born in May–June after 225–270 days' gestation. **9c**

Black rat   *Rattus rattus*   RODENTIA

Originally a native of South-East Asia, the black rat has now spread throughout the world.

The body of a fully grown male is about 18cm long and the tail is notably longer — between 20 and 23cm. The head is pointed with small ears and large whiskers. The colour varies from black to dark brown above, sometimes with grey, and the under parts are yellowish grey to light brown.

It is probably one of the greatest pests to farmers and owners of stored foodstuffs and it can transmit bubonic plague and other diseases. There may be 5–6 litters a year, each of 5–8 young. It reaches sexual maturity at 11 weeks. **9d**

European wild cat   *Felis silvestris*   CARNIVORA
Once common in most forested areas of the British Isles, the wild cat is now restricted to the Scottish highlands. It is also found in the remoter areas of France, the Balkans, eastern Europe and central Asia.

It is similar in appearance to a domestic cat but larger, up to 91cm long overall, and with a shorter head and a shorter tail which is the same thickness throughout its length. The fur is light yellow grey with poorly defined black stripes and the tail is ringed with black and has a black tip. The whiskers are long.

The wild cat feeds on game birds, rabbit, hares and other small mammals. It lives alone except during the mating season. 4–5 kittens are born after 68 days' gestation. **9e**

Otter   *Lutra lutra*   CARNIVORA
The otter ranges almost throughout Europe, the British Isles, parts of Asia and northern Africa. It lives in or on the banks of streams and lakes, digging a burrow with several entrances.

A member of the weasel family, it is adapted for an aquatic life. The long slender body is about 76cm long and the tail, which is about 46cm long, is thick at the root and flattened towards the tip. The head is broad and flattened with small rounded ears, which can be closed under water, and a pointed muzzle with sensitive whiskers. The legs are short and the feet webbed with short curved claws.

It feeds on fish, crayfish, frogs and, occasionally, game birds and small mammals. Mating occurs in the water, at any season, and 2–3 cubs are born after about 8 weeks' gestation. **9f**

Pipistrelle bat   *Pipistrellus pipistrellus*   CHIROPTERA
This bat ranges over most of Europe and much of Asia, eastward to Japan and Korea, and is to be found in buildings and hollow trees.

The head and body are only 2.5–5cm long with a tail of 2.5cm. The body is fairly stout with a broad head and a blunt muzzle. The ears are triangular in shape. The wing span is up to 21.5cm. The fur is silky and varies in colour from yellowish brown to dark brown above, with slightly lighter under parts and blackish brown wings and ears.

It is one of the earliest bats to be seen, appearing at the end of March. It feeds on insects and hibernates about the end of October. The gestation period is 34–44 days and a single offspring is born in July. **10a**

Eurasian badger   *Meles meles*   CARNIVORA
The badger is found throughout most of Europe, including the British Isles, and extends eastwards to Japan.

It has a stout heavily built body, about 75cm long, and a tail of a further 10–15cm. The legs are short and the feet have strong curved claws for digging. A bony ridge runs along the centre of the skull. The coat is grey above and black below and on the legs. The head is white with two prominent black stripes extending through the eye and ear regions. The ears have white tips.

The badger feeds on earthworms, insects, slugs, snails, young rabbits and small mammals as well as fruit, cereals, acorns and bulbs. The burrow, or sett, generally has more than one entrance and here the cubs, usually 2–3, are born in January–April. Their eyes may not open until they are 5 weeks old and they first come above ground after 8–9 weeks. **10b**

Roe deer   *Capreolus capreolus*   ARTIODACTYLA
This small deer is found in the British Isles and much of northern Europe and Asia.

The buck is 66–76cm in high at the shoulder and has small 3-tined antlers, which rarely exceed 23–25cm and rise nearly vertically from the skull. These are shed every year. The head is fairly short, with medium-sized ears and a sharp muzzle. The neck is slender. The rufous summer coat becomes greyish fawn in winter and a white tail patch appears.

The roe deer feeds in family groups, on grasses and vegetation, at dawn and dusk. Rutting takes place in July and the does give birth to the white-spotted fawns, usually 1–2, in the following Spring. **10c**

European hedgehog   *Erinaceus europaeus*   INSECTIVORA
The hedgehog is a common sight in the Biritish Isles and in many parts of Europe.

Under 30cm long, with a tail of about 2.5cm, it has a pig-like snout, small rounded ears and a body covered with a thick coat of short spines. When the hedgehog is rolled into a ball, these provide a formidable defence. The legs are short and the 5 toes of each foot all bear short claws.

The hedgehog remains under the cover of vegetation during the day, emerging at dusk to feed on insects, worms and snails. Berries and fruits, frogs, toads, reptiles and birds' eggs are also eaten. It hibernates in a nest of leaves. 3–6 young are born in late summer. Their spines do not harden for several days. **10d**

Wood mouse *Apodemus sylvaticus* RODENTIA
This species, also known as the long-tailed field mouse, is common in the British Isles and is widely distributed over most of Europe and parts of Asia. Local races often occur.

The head and body are about 9cm long and the tail is almost as long again. The coat is fawn above and white below. The colour and large hind feet distinguish it from the house mouse. The ears and eyes are comparatively large and the muzzle is long and pointed.

The wood mouse burrows just below the ground and feeds on cereals, root crops, seeds and nuts, some of which are stored for the winter. The female gives birth to 4–9 young up to 4 times a year. **10e**

Red fox *Vulpes vulpes vulpes* CARNIVORA
This fox is found practically all over Europe, including the British Isles, and also in most of Asia.

A member of the dog family, it is about 60–76cm long with a bushy tail, or brush, of about 38–46cm. The body is slender, reddish brown above and white below, with black on the backs of the ears and legs. The muzzle is pointed and the ears large and erect.

It leaves its earth at night to hunt for mice, rabbits, birds, insects and fruit. The young, usually 3–8 in number, are born in late spring or early summer after a gestation period of 61–63 days. **10f**

European mole *Talpa europaea* INSECTIVORA
The mole is widely distributed throughout Eurasia, including the British Isles.

About 12–15cm long, with a tiny tail of another few centimetres, the mole has a long shrew-like snout and short legs. The ears are very small and the tiny eyes are almost buried in the fur, which is generally black. The feet are naked and flesh-coloured with strong curved claws. The fore feet are positioned well in front of the body to facilitate digging.

The mole feeds mainly on earthworms and lives mainly under ground in a complex system of tunnels radiating from a central breeding chamber. The young are born in late spring or early summer, usually 3–5, after a gestation period of 42 days. **10g**

MEDITERRANEAN SCRUB

European polecat   *Mustela putorius putorius*   CARNIVORA
The polecat ranges over most of Europe and is distinguishable by its size and offensive smell.

A fully grown male is about 71cm long with a tail of about 20cm. The head is pointed with a sharp nose and rounded ears. The body is long and slender and the fur consists of long blackish brown guard hairs and pale creamy brown, woolly under fur. The short legs are black and a black band runs along the under side of the body.

It is a voracious predator of rats, hares and rabbits, game birds, lizards, snakes, fish and eggs, which it mostly hunts at night. A litter of 3–8 young is produced in April–May after 40–60 days' gestation. There may be a second litter later in the year. **11a**

Mouflon   *Ovis musimon*   ARTIODACTYLA
Originally from the forests of Corsica and Sardinia, this species has now been introduced into many parts of southern and central Europe.

The mouflon is 107–127cm long with a tail of about 5cm. It stands 63–76cm at the shoulder with pale areas on the flanks and parts of the head, legs and belly and a pale rump patch. The long powerful horns of the male grow to a length of 50–81cm and curve backwards. The female sometimes has short horns.

It lives in flocks and feeds on grasses, sedges and herbaceous plants. Mating occurs in late autumn and, after about 5 months' gestation, 1–3 lambs are produced. **11b**

Fallow deer   *Dama dama*   ARTIODACTYLA
The fallow deer is native to countries bordering the Mediterranean but has also been introduced to the British Isles.

The male, which is a little larger than the female, is about 90cm high at the shoulder. The ears are large and the tail is larger than in most deer. The characteristic antlers are rounded at the base but get wider as they rise and end in a flattened palmate upper part with snags on the trailing edge. they may be up to 76cm long. The coat is reddish fawn in summer with a dark dorsal stripe and white spots, white on the belly and part of the tail. In winter the spots disappear and the coat is a greyish brown.

Rut occurs in the autumn and the doe produces usually 1, but sometimes 2–3, fawns the following May–June. **11c**

Rabbit   *Oryctolagus cuniculus*   LAGOMORPHA
The rabbit is common throughout Europe and has given rise to most of the domesticated breeds.

It is smaller than the hare, weighing up to 2.25kg and measuring up to 46cm long. The ears are shorter than those of the hare, with no black tips, while the fur is brownish grey with black speckles and a rufous tinge on the neck. The tail is short, black above and white beneath.

The rabbit is a gregarious burrowing animal. A group of burrows is known as a warren. The young are born after only 4 weeks' gestation and can themselves reproduce at 6 months. **11d**

Mole-rat   *Spalax microphthalmus*   RODENTIA
The mole-rat is native to the eastern Mediterranean and, although originally found in steppe regions, now inhabits riverbanks and roadsides.

It is totally blind with no external eye openings and is seldom seen above ground. The body is 18–28cm long and it weighs up to 225g. The back is grey-brown with a reddish tinge. Using its teeth, head and feet, the mole-rat digs an intricate tunnel system which connects with those of its neighbours.

Active mainly from late afternoon to early morning, the mole-rat feeds on tree roots and herbaceous plants. There is only 1 litter a year, of 4–5 young, born in spring. **11e**

EVERGREEN FOREST: ASIA

Red panda   *Ailurus fulgens*   CARNIVORA
The red panda lives in the mountain forests of Nepal, Sikkim, Yunnan, Szechwan and upper Burma.

It resembles a large cat with a raccoon-like tail, bushy and thick with contrasting rings of colour, about 40–50cm long. The body is about 60cm long, covered with thick soft fur, rusty red above and black below. The stout legs are also black and the feet have sharp curved claws which are partially retractile. The face is white except for 2 dark streaks running from the eyes to the corners of the mouth.

The diet of young shoots, leaves and fruits may be supplemented by the occasional bird's egg. The young, usually 2, are born in spring. They remain with the parents for about 1 year. **12a**

Giant panda *Ailuropoda melanoleuca* CARNIVORA
The giant panda is a solitary animal frequenting the bamboo forests of south-west China and it is now extremely rare. Despite its bear-like appearance it is probably more closely related to the raccoons.

A fully grown panda is about 152cm long with a short tail of a further 13cm. It weighs between 90 and 136kg. The long coat is white except for the legs, arms, upper chest and across the shoulders, the ears and the 'spectacles' around the eyes.

The panda feeds throughout the day on bamboo shoots and stems. An elongated bone on each fore foot acts as a sixth claw which assists grasping. Little is known of breeding in the wild. **12b**

Tahr *Hemitragus jemlahicus* ARTIODACTYLA
This wild goat inhabits the forested areas of the mountains of southern Asia.

It stands about 90cm high at the shoulder and has a long narrow face. The head is covered in very short fur, although the male has a long soft mane. The small horns are set close together. Both sexes are reddish brown in colour.

The tahr lives in herds which move over the slopes, feeding on grass and vegetation during the morning and evening and resting in the afternoon. The young are born in June–July after 6 months' gestation. **12c**

Chinese water deer *Hydropotes inermis* ARTIODACTYLA
This deer lives in swampy reed beds in China and Korea but has been introduced to the British Isles and France.

A small deer, 76–99cm long, with a tail of 5–7.5cm, it stands 43–53cm high at the shoulder. The coat, which has remarkable insulating properties, is a uniform yellow-brown with dark flecks. Neither sex possesses antlers but, in both, the upper canines are elongated to form tusks. It has a number of scent glands, including one in front of each eye.

With its characteristic hare-like movement, this deer is active both night and day, feeding on grasses and other plants. The young, usually 3–7 in number, are born in May–June. **12d**

Chinese muntjac deer   *Muntiacus reevesi*   ARTIODACTYLA
The muntjac, or barking deer, lives in woodland with dense undergrowth in south and eastern Asia but has been introduced to the British Isles and France.

It is about 79–99cm long and stands 43cm high at the shoulder. The tail is about 15cm long. The coat is short and soft, varying in colour from pale brown to red-brown. The male has short antlers (15cm) borne on high hairy pedicles. The upper canines are slightly elongated and directed outwards.

Grasses, leaves, shoots and buds form its diet. Rutting probably occurs towards the end of summer and 1–2 young are born after 6 months' gestation. **12e**

EVERGREEN FOREST: AUSTRALIA

Sugar glider   *Petaurus sciureus*   MARSUPIALIA
The sugar glider comes from eastern Australia.

Over all the animal is 46–51cm long. The tail, which is non-prehensile and bushy, is about the same length as the body. The fur is ashy grey above with a chestnut-coloured streak running along the centre of the back from the top of the nose to the root of the tail. The under parts are yellowish white, there are blackish rings around the eyes and the bases of the ears and the cheeks are white with a black patch below the ear. The broad gliding membrane is brownish with a white edge and stretches from the wrist of the fore foot to the ankle of the hind foot.

It lives mainly in gum trees and is nocturnal, feeding on leaves and small insects. **13a**

Great glider   *Schoinobates volans*   MARSUPIALIA
This marsupial occurs in eastern Australia from Queensland to Victoria.

It is about 43cm long and the tail, of about 50cm, is bushy with a small area of naked skin on the under surface at the tip. The head is squirrel-like with short, rounded ears and a pointed muzzle. The fur is generally black or blackish brown above and white below. There is a membrane joining the fore and hind limbs on either side of the body by means of which it can glide through the air.

In habit it is both nocturnal and arboreal. It sleeps curled up in a gum tree during the day and, at dusk, planes and leaps between the branches, feeding on gum leaves and other vegetation. **13b**

Eastern native cat *Dasyurus quoll* MARSUPIALIA
This carnivore, also known as a quoll, is found in south-eastern Australia, Tasmania and New Guinea.

About the size of a domestic cat, it is 41–46cm long with a furry tail of about 30cm, tipped with white. The body is slender with a marten-like head, a pointed muzzle and long, narrow, pointed ears. The fur is generally olive-grey with conspicuous white spots. The belly is pale grey.

A solitary terrestrial animal, it feeds at night on birds and birds' eggs, small mammals and insects. The female gives birth to a litter of up to 8, usually in May. The young are independent at 4 months. 13c

Dingo *Canis dingo* CARNIVORA
It is uncertain whether the dingo is indigenous to Australia or whether it was introduced as a tame species and has since become wild. It frequents the more wooded parts of the country.

Smaller than the wolf, the dingo has a short broad muzzle, large pointed ears and moderately long legs. The tail is bushy, especially towards the tip, which is usually whitish. The general colouration of the body varies from sandy yellow to, in some cases, almost brownish black above, and white to yellowish brown below. The feet are often white.

Nocturnal in habit, it hunts in small packs or family groups, preying on small livestock, especially sheep. 13d

Wombat *Vombatus ursinus* MARSUPIALIA
This species comes from Tasmania and islands in the Bass Strait, where it lives in burrows and rock crevices, emerging to feed at night. It is related to the hairy wombat and the common wombat of the south of Australia.

It is a stout, heavily built animal, about 90cm long, with a broad flattened head, short rounded ears, small eyes, a stumpy tail and short legs. The toes of the fore feet have 5 strong, curved digging claws. The fur is short, coarse and greyish brown and was once much sought after. The wombat is now a protected species.

The teeth are rootless and the incisors are chisel-like and adapted for gnawing the bark, roots and grasses which form the wombat's chief food. The female gives birth to a single offspring. 13e

Rabbit bandicoot *Thylacomys lagotis* MARSUPIALIA
This rabbit-sized marsupial, known also as the bilby, and characterised by its large ears, lives in scattered populations in Western and

South Australia and parts of New South Wales.

The body is about 46cm long, covered in soft silky fur, pale grey on the back and white on the belly. The tail, which is about 23cm long, has a crest of hair on the rear third and a white tip. The head is long and pointed. Of the 4 toes on each elongated hind foot, the second and third are fused. The small fore feet each have 5 toes.

These burrowing animals normally live in pairs and emerge at dusk to feed on roots, insects and other small animals. **13f**

Tasmanian devil   *Sarcophilus harrissii*   MARSUPIALIA
This animal is now restricted to Tasmania, where it lives in rock crevices and caves.

It is a stoutly built carnivore, somewhat similar to a badger, with a broad head and a short muzzle. It is about 71cm long, with a thickly furred tail about 30cm long. The ears are fairly short and rounded. The limbs are also short, the fore feet with 5 toes and the hind feet with 4 toes, all with powerful claws. It is black or blackish brown in colour with a white collar, a white area on the rump and, sometimes, white lateral spots on the shoulders. It emerges at dusk to hunt almost any of the smaller mammals and birds.

Mating is in March and April and the young are born, 3–4 at a birth, in May. These spend their early days in the pouch. **13g**

Koala   *Phascolarctos cinereus*   MARSUPIALIA
The koala is found in the eastern parts of Queensland, New South Wales and Victoria.

It is a short, thick-set, tail-less marsupial, about 80cm long. The wide bear-like head has large, roundish ears with a thick fringe of fur. The eyes are small and the nose naked and bulbous. The feet have large, curved claws, well adapted for climbing trees. The first and second toes of the fore feet are opposable to the remaining 3. On the hind feet, only the first toe is opposable. The thick woolly fur is dark grey above, yellowish white on the hindquarters and greyish white on the belly.

The koala lives alone or in a small group and is arboreal and nocturnal. It feeds on the leaves and shoots of the eucalyptus. Mating occurs between September and January and the gestation period is 35 days. Births are usually single. **14a**

Brush-tailed opossum   *Trichosurus vulpecula*   MARSUPIALIA
This marsupial is found in Tasmania and most of Australia except for the central regions.

About the size of a fox, it has a pointed head and long ears which are hairy at the back. The thick woolly fur, which is silvery grey above and yellowish white below, varying to a reddish hue, and the prehensile bushy tail, are characteristic of the species. The legs are more or less equal in length, unlike those of the larger marsupials. The feet are 5-toed and the fore feet are furnished with sharp claws.

It lives in tree holes during the day, emerging at night to feed on leaves, buds and fruits and, occasionally, small birds. It is also found in towns. The female gives birth to a single young which remains in the pouch until it can cling to her back. **14b**

Banded numbat   *Myrmecobius fasciatus*   MARSUPIALIA
This squirrel-like marsupial is restricted to parts of South and Western Australia. It is also known as the banded or marsupial anteater.

The body is about 25cm long and the tail about 18cm. The head is long and broad, with a narrow, pointed muzzle and short oval ears. A dark stripe runs through each eye. The head and body are reddish chestnut above with transverse bands of white on the lower back and hindquarters. The belly is yellowish brown. The fore feet have 5 clawed toes whilst the hind feet have only 4.

The tongue is very long and sticky and used for licking up termites and ants. The female is pouched and gives birth to 4 young during January–March. **14c**

Brush-tailed phascogale   *Phascogale tapoatafa*   MARSUPIALIA
This genus of small carnivorous marsupials is characterised by the length of the tail, which is nearly as long as the body and is evenly tufted towards the tip. An adult is about 43cm long overall. The head is rat-like, with large erect ears and a pointed muzzle. The body is stoutly built with coarse greyish fur above and white fur below. A prominent black streak runs vertically down the nose.

The phascogale, sometimes called the brush-tailed marsupial mouse, feeds on insects, mice, lizards, small birds and birds' eggs. There are usually 6–8 young in a litter. The female has 10 teats but the pouch is rudimentary, consisting of loose folds of skin rather than a true pouch. **14d**

Tasmanian wolf   *Thylacinus cynocephalus*   MARSUPIALIA
The largest of the carnivorous marsupials, this animal, also known as the thylacine or pouched wolf, is now restricted to Tasmania and is extremely rare.

The body of a fully grown male is about 106cm long, with a

tapering non-prehensile tail about 53cm long. It is covered with greyish brown fur marked with transverse bands of black across the saddle, rump and loins and root of the tail. It is rather dog-like, with a pointed muzzle and medium-sized erect ears. The limbs are about equal in length. The fore feet have 5 toes and the hind feet have 4, all with short blunt claws.

The female bears up to 4 young at a time, which are carried in the pouch. **14e**

Duck-billed platypus   *Ornithorhynchus anatinus*   MONOTREMATA
The platypus is found in south-eastern Australia and Tasmania where it lives in a burrow, with an underwater entrance, on the banks of lakes or rivers in forest clearings.

About 46cm long, with another 13–15cm of tail, it has a stout body covered with short, soft dark brown fur, rather like a mole. The head is broad and the unique duck-like bill is covered with skin and has small nostrils near the tip. The eyes and ears are barely perceptible. The short limbs have webbed feet, the web being more pronounced on the fore feet, and the tail is broad and flattened — to facilitate swimming.

The platypus feeds mainly on small crustaceans, worm and aquatic insects. Unlike other mammals, the young are hatched from eggs, normally laid 2 at a time at the end of the burrow. They are suckled after birth. **14f**

4
Grasslands

There are two types of grassland, temperate and tropical, and the animals which inhabit them have many features in common.

The temperate grasslands are found in the middle latitudes of the Northern Hemisphere and the lower latitudes of the Southern Hemisphere. They are variously known: as *steppes* in the USSR, *prairies* in North America, *pampas* in South America and *veldt* in South Africa. In Australia and China respectively there are the Murray-Darling and Manchurian Plains.

Rainfall in these grasslands is about 25–75cm per year, but it falls mainly in spring and early summer, when evaporation is highest, and consequently much of it is lost. The temperature range is considerable, particularly in the Northern Hemisphere, where it may fluctuate from $-15°C$ in winter to $32°C$ in summer. The range is smaller in the Southern Hemisphere because of the moderating influence of the sea.

The rich soil, known as *chernozem*, supports a rolling grassland, although scarcity of water restricts tree growth to a few willows, alders and poplars along water courses. The grasses are coarse and wiry with parallel veins, greyish green in colour and able to curl their blades inwards to conserve water. Height varies with water availability. Propagation is often by underground shoots or surface runners and some species grow from their bases rather than their tips. This prevents damage by overgrazing.

The tropical grasslands or savannas occur between the deserts and the equatorial forests, generally between the Tropics of Cancer and Capricorn. They are found in the interior of northern Australia, in Africa and in South America. The wetter, low-lying savannas in South America are known as *llanos* and the drier ones, in the uplands, as *campos*. The stretches of savanna in India are largely the result of forest clearance.

The temperature range in the savanna is small. Winter temperatures average $21°C$ and summer temperatures may exceed $32°C$. Rainfall may be as high as 150cm a year, but, again, most of it is lost by evaporation as it falls mainly in the summer months.

There is a gradation of vegetation, from poor grass with scattered thorn bushes near the desert margin, through grass of increasing richness, which, although often dry in appearance, may reach 1.5–3m in height, to increasingly dense woodland as the forest margin is reached.

The grasslands, particularly those of the tropics, support a great number and variety of animals, although different groups are predominant in different continents: marsupials in Australia, hooved animals in Africa and rodents in South America. Most of these animals are herbivores.

Because of the open nature of grassland, the larger animals would be seen easily if it were not for their colouring. Generally they are lighter below than above, which gives them a very flat appearance. Patches of colour, stripes and blotches tend to break up the outline, so that the animals' shapes are recognised less easily and the animals merge into the shadows of tall grasses or light tree cover.

Speed is an important means of escape for many species. The hooved animals have long muscular legs, whereas the kangaroos, wallabies and many rodents have greatly developed hind legs for leaping. They are all capable of sustained speed. The carnivores can run at much greater speeds but for short distances only.

Hearing and eye-sight are generally keen, as danger can be sensed from a long way off. In order to see further, many animals, particularly small rodents, habitually sit on their haunches. The prairie marmot and viscacha even build mounds around the entrances to their burrows for this reason.

Special defence mechanisms exist in some species, e.g. the spines of the porcupine and the scales of the pangolins and armadillos. The horns in many hooved animals may be used as weapons, but usually as a last resort.

The herding instinct is common among herbivores, from the guinea pig of the pampas to the wildebeeste of the African plains. Weight of numbers is a considerable defence and also increases the chances of an early warning. The social structures, seen in the lion for the care of the young rather than for protection, become very elaborate in species such as the marmot and the yellow baboon and are an important factor in survival.

Burrowing is adopted by many of the smaller animals, for concealment, breeding, and to avoid temperature extremes. In the tropical grasslands, the aardvark and ratel, among others, avoid the heat of the day by retiring underground. On the steppes, the hamster and the souslik retire to their burrows to avoid the winter frosts and snows.

Many animals, if they do not seek a burrow, rest up during the day, feeding at dawn and dusk, or during the night. The herbivores of the grasslands are selective about their food, taking particular types of plants or plants at different stages of development. Thus the tiny dik dik feeds on the very lowest branches, the gerenuk stands on its hind legs to browse higher up and the giraffe takes the topmost leaves of the trees. Competition for food sources is thus reduced. To extract the maximum value from their food source, the digestive systems of herbivores are modified to various degrees, from a simple lengthening of the small intestine to the complex four-chambered stomach of the ruminants – the cattle, deer, antelopes, sheep, goats, giraffes and okapi.

NORTH AMERICA

Spotted skunk *Spilogale putorius* CARNIVORA
The spotted skunk is found in southern North America, south to Panama.

Its long soft fur is black with white stripes or random white patches. Unlike other skunks, it can climb trees. For defence, it discharges an offensive fluid from its anal glands.

It lives in nests of dry vegetation in burrows under rocks and feeds on insects, mice, eggs, birds and vegetation. 4–8 young are born in the spring after 50–60 days' gestation. **15a**

Pronghorn *Antilocapra americana* ARTIODACTYLA
The pronghorn has characteristics of both the antelopes and the goats, as its Latin name suggests. It lives in herds on the open plains of western North America and is now a protected species.

It stands about 107cm at the shoulder and is brown above, with a slight mane on the neck and a darker brown face. There are prominent white patches on the cheeks and throat, and the under parts, flanks and rump are also white. The horns rise vertically from the head with an outward curve, recurving at the tips with a single branch, or snag, projecting forward about halfway up the stem. The outer sheath is shed annually. **15b**

American bison *Bison bison* ARTIODACTYLA
Once numerous in central and western North America, the bison was once hunted almost to extinction. It is now strictly preserved.

It is powerfully built, with a massive bearded head, humped shoulders, short (35–40cm) curved round horns, relatively small hooves and a short, bushy-tipped tail. An average bull is 152cm high at the shoulders. The coat is thick and luxuriant on the head, neck and shoulders, and often on the fore legs, but is thinner on the flanks. It is dark brown and even darker on the head and throat. The coat is shed from February to midsummer and is at its best in December.

A single calf is born at a time. The coat is yellowish brown at first becoming darker with age. **15c**

Black-tailed prairie marmot   *Cynomys ludovicianius*   RODENTIA
This species of marmot, also known as the prairie dog because of its characteristic barking alarm cry, was once widespread in the plains of central North America.

It is a stout-bodied rodent, about 33cm long, with a short bushy tail. The coat is pale brown in colour, becoming paler on the under side. In habit, it resembles other marmot species.

It feeds during the day on a variety of vegetation. A colonial animal, the prairie dog lives in one of many small family groups which together form a 'town'. This is a complex underground burrowing system which may extend for several miles. Raised lips around the burrow entrances prevent flooding and provide 'look-out posts'. **15d**

Coyote   *Canis latrans*   CARNIVORA
The coyote is found over most of the western plains of North America and as far south as Central America.

It is closely related to the wolf and jackal, about 91cm long and weighing up to 18kg. The coat is thicker than that of the wolf and the tail is very bushy. Colour varies according to season and locality but is generally yellowish grey, with touches of reddish yellow on the neck and legs and whitish under parts.

It lives alone or in pairs and feeds on small rodents, rabbits, some fruit and vegetables, and carrion. The gestation period is 60–64 days and there are 5–6 cubs in a litter. **15e**

American badger   *Taxidea taxus*   CARNIVORA
This badger is found in southern Canada and the northern USA and as far west as Montana and Wyoming.

It is about 76cm long with a tail of a further 10cm. An adult male weighs up to 12kg but the female is distinctly smaller. The coat is reddish brown to greyish in colour with a bold white stripe from the nose to the shoulders. There are black patches on the cheeks and the feet are dark brown. The under parts vary from whitish to pale reddish buff.

The badger digs extensive burrow systems and feeds on small mammals, frogs, snakes and insects. After mating in August and September, 1–5 cubs are born in April–June. **15f**

EURASIA

Brown hare   *Lepus europaeus*   LAGOMORPHA
The brown hare is found in most parts of northern Europe, including the British Isles, and its range extends eastwards into south-west Asia. It generally lives in flat open country.

An adult is 38–68cm long, with a tail of a further 5–10cm, and weighs 2.5–6.4kg. The coat is greyish to reddish brown with a speckled appearance due to the black-tipped hairs. The hind legs and feet are long in proportion to the body and the ears are long with black tips.

The hare spends the day in its 'form' – a depression in the ground, and feeds after sunset on grass, clover, cereals, root vegetables and tree bark. There are 3–4 litters a year, each of 2–5 young. **16a**

Water vole   *Arvicola terrestris*   RODENTIA
The water vole occurs throughout Europe, except for south and western France, the Iberian peninsula and certain other southern areas, and its range extends eastward into Asia. In the north it is associated with water and dense vegetation, in the south with grassland.

It is 13–23cm long, with a 5–10cm tail, although the size varies according to locality. It can be distinguished from the rat by the short broad head, blunt muzzle and the unobtrusive small ears. The thick glossy fur is dark to reddish or greyish brown.

It lives in burrows and feeds on grass and also seeds, bulbs, roots and bark. It has 2–4 litters a year, each of 4–8 young. **16b**

European souslik   *Citellus citellus*   RODENTIA
This small rodent is a member of the squirrel family. Its range includes much of central and eastern Europe, extending into northern Asia and Siberia.

It is about 20cm long, with a short tail of about 7cm. The fur is dark reddish brown above and reddish yellow below. There is a white patch on the chin and the throat is also whitish. It has cheek pouches for storing food, the ears are very small and the eyes are encircled with yellow. The souslik is gregarious and lives in a burrow, which forms part of a colony, where it hibernates. There are usually 4–8 young in a litter. **16c**

Common hamster   *Cricetus cricetus*   RODENTIA
The common hamster is found from western Europe to Siberia but does not occur in the British Isles.

It is the largest hamster with a stoutish body 20–30cm long and a short stumpy tail. The head is relatively large with a pointed muzzle, the eyes are large and the ears somewhat rounded. It has large cheek pouches for food storage. The fur is reddish brown above and black below with white markings on the sides. The feet are white and furnished with small claws.

It feeds on grain, fruit, roots and bulbs, mainly at night. It lives in an elaborate burrow system where it overwinters from about October to March. 5–18 young are born after a gestation of 20–22 days. **16d**

Saiga   *Saiga tatarica*   ARTIODACTYLA
This sheep-like antelope lives in the steppe country of the southern USSR.

It stands about 76cm high at the shoulder. The male has amber yellow horns about 30cm long. The most distinctive features are the swollen muzzle and downward-pointing nostrils. The ears and eyes are large and there are scent glands behind the knees and under the eyes.

The herds of 5–45 females, led by a male, migrate in winter. They feed on shrubs and grasses. Females mature very early and 1–3 young are born in May after about 6 months' gestation. **16e**

ASIA

Persian lynx   *Felis caracal*   CARNIVORA
The Persian lynx or caracal is found in arid regions ranging from western India, through south-western Asia and Arabia and extending into Africa.

It differs from the northern lynx in several respects. The body, which is about 60cm long, is much more streamlined, the tail is longer (25cm) and the legs are longer and more slender. It is 40–46cm high at the shoulder. The soft, thick coat is generally sandy brown in colour with lighter under parts and is sometimes spotted. The ears are large and triangular with tufts of long black hair at the tips and the eyes are large.

It feeds sometimes on small mammals but usually on birds and can leap 3m from the ground to catch its prey. Except in the breeding season, this lynx is solitary. The female gives birth to 2–4 young after 9 weeks' gestation. **17a**

Indian pangolin   *Manis crassicaudata*   PHOLIDOTA
The Indian pangolin is found in southern Asia. Like all pangolins, it has a long tapering body covered in overlapping scales, except on the snout and under parts. These scales are a form of hair. The tail is very broad and heavy and prehensile. The fore feet are furnished with 5 strong claws which are a powerful aid to digging.

The pangolin feeds on ants and termites and has a long (30cm) tongue and no teeth. It is nocturnal; during the day it sleeps in a burrow up to 3m deep. In late winter, 1–2 young are born. **17b**

Indian grey mongoose   *Herpestes edwardsi*   CARNIVORA
The grey mongoose is found throughout most of the Indian peninsula and Sir Lanka (Ceylon), westwards to Arabia.

It is a weasel-like animal about 38–46cm long, with a tail of 35–38cm, a pointed muzzle, a rather short nose and short rounded ears. The legs are quite short and each foot has 5 toes with long straight claws. The long coarse fur is a uniform grey or rufous colour, darker on the legs. It eats birds, lizards, insects, fruit and rats and is well known for its ability to attack and kill snakes.

In the spring, 3–4 young are born after a gestation of about 60 days. **17c**

Blackbuck   *Antilope cervicapra*   ARTIODACTYLA
The blackbuck ranges over the grassy plains of India, not far from water, in herds of 50–60 animals, headed by an adult male.

It is about 122cm long and stands up to 81cm at the shoulder. The horns occur only in the male. Close together at the base, they diverge as they rise in a ringed corkscrew to a length of 76cm or so. They are much prized by sportsmen. The coat is greyish or blackish brown above and white below and there is a distinctive white ring around each eye. The females and young are fawn-coloured above. **17d**

Nilgai   *Boselaphus tragocamelus*   ARTIODACTYLA
The nilgai or blue bull is one of the largest of the Indian antelopes and is found in dry open forest and savanna.

It stands 137cm high at the shoulder. The male has small, smooth, slightly curved horns up to 23cm long, and a smooth bluish grey coat.

The female is more brownish in colour. Both sexes have a small neck mane and patches of white on the ears, nose, legs and throat. The male has a black ruff below the throat patch.

The nilgai moves in herds, grazing and also taking browse from shrubs. 1–2 young are born after 247 days' gestation. **17e**

Cheetah   *Acinonyx jubatus*   CARNIVORA

The cheetah has a wide range, from southern Asia, where it is now very rare, to many parts of Africa south of the Sahara. It lives mainly in open grassland.

It is about 228cm long, including a 76cm tail, and stands about 76cm at the shoulder. The fur is yellow, heavily marked on the body, legs and upper tail with dark blackish brown spots. The end of the tail is ringed alternately with yellow and blackish brown and has a white tip. The under parts are white and the face has a white muzzle with a black streak extending from mouth to eye. The ears are small and rounded.

Its long legs enable it to chase its prey (antelopes and other medium-sized mammals) at great speed. **17f**

SOUTH AMERICA

Pampas deer   *Ozotoceras bezoarticus*   ARTIODACTYLA

This deer is the only native ruminant on the pampas and is found from central Brazil south to Argentina.

It is a small deer, standing about 68cm high at the shoulder. The coat is yellowish brown above and paler on the under side. Antlers are found only in the male and have up to 6 tines.

It lives in pairs or small herds, feeding mainly on grasses. Habitat destruction has seriously reduced its numbers. **18a**

Hairy armadillo   *Chaetophractus villosus*   EDENTATA

The hairy armadillo is found in South America to the east of the Andes and south of the Amazon Basin.

It is about 50cm long, excluding the tail, and, like all armadillos, bears an armour of bony scales. These form immovable shields in the shoulder and pelvic regions and a series of flexible bands along the back. This species characteristically has many long hairs projecting from between the dorsal bands. The face and under side are soft and covered with hair. The front feet bear powerful claws for digging and the tongue is long, extensile and sticky.

This armadillo feeds on insects, fruit, worms, small vertebrates and carrion. It escapes from danger by running, pressing itself close to the ground or burrowing. **18b**

Maned wolf   *Chrysocyon brachyurus*   CARNIVORA
The maned wolf is found in the grasslands of southern Brazil, Paraguay and northern Argentina.

It is similar to a fox but has extremely long legs. The body is covered with long soft hair of a rich reddish brown. The throat and tail tip are white but the feet and legs are black. The erectile mane on the neck is also black.

Except during the mating season, the wolf is solitary. It feeds at night on guinea pigs, rabbits, viscachas, birds, insects, reptiles and fruit. **18c**

Burmeister's fairy armadillo   *Burmeisteria retusa*   EDENTATA
This is one of the small fairy armadillos and is native to eastern Bolivia and northern Argentina where it is found in the more arid areas of the grasslands.

Also known as the greater pichiciego, it is 13–18cm long. The pinkish brown scales are less bony than in other armadillos and form a series of plates from the nose, across the head and back, and a separate tail plate at the rear, which acts as a plug when the animal is in its burrow. The small tail protrudes below the tail plate. Where there are no scales, the armadillo is covered in long, white, silky hairs. The eyes and ears are very small but the feet and front claws are very powerful.

This armadillo spends most of its time underground and burrowing is the chief means of defence. It feeds on insects and worms and the occasional small vertebrate. **18d**

Giant anteater   *Myrmecophaga tridactyla*   EDENTATA
The giant anteater is found in swampy savanna throughout tropical Central and South America from Guatemala to Paraguay.

It is about 122cm long with a tail of about the same length covered in hair more than 30cm long. It stands about 60cm high at the shoulder. The body is covered in greyish black hair, which forms a crest along the neck and back, and there are distinctive black and white markings running from the throat to the middle of the body. The snout is long and tapering, with a small mouth and a long sticky tongue for extracting ants from their nests.

The anteater is nocturnal, spending the day in its lair in long grasses. A single young is born. **18e**

Mara (Patagonian hare)   *Dolichotis patagona*   RODENTIA
The mara or Patagonian hare is a member of the guinea pig family and is found in the pampas of Argentina and the stony wastes of Patagonia.

It is 60–90cm long and 30cm high at the shoulder. The coat is pale and sandy with a conspicuous white rump patch which acts as a warning signal. The back is darker. Long lashes protect the eyes from the sun and the ears are large.

The mara lives in groups of about 15. It is active during the day, eating grasses, roots and stems, and retires to its burrow at night. When alarmed it moves quickly on its long legs, with a peculiar gait known as 'stotting'. The female produces 2 litters of 2–5 young a year. **19a**

Pampas fox   *Dusicyon gymnocerus*   CARNIVORA
The pampas fox or Azara's dog is found on the pampas and southern campos of Brazil.

It is slightly smaller than the red fox and the coat is more golden brown in colour, with darker markings on the face. The muzzle is shorter and the ears are relatively large and rounded. The sense of hearing is acute.

It lives in open country, where there is a cover of tall grasses, and holes up in dens taken over from viscachas and armadillos. It is omnivorous, feeding on fruit as well as small rodents, birds, reptiles and insects. **19b**

Plains viscacha   *Lagostomus maximus*   RODENTIA
The viscacha lives on the pampas of Argentina and Patagonia, in warrens characterised by the mounded openings to the burrows. It fills the same ecological niche as the marmots of North America.

It is about 50cm long, including a 20cm tail, and is heavily built with a very large head. The short soft fur is dark grey and the face is marked with black and white. The male has a long moustache.

The viscacha generally feeds in the evening, chiefly on grasses and seeds but also on roots. **19c**

Tucotuco   *Ctenomys brasiliensis*   RODENTIA
The tucotuco is found in the south of South America.

It is a small stocky rodent about 25cm long with a tail of about 10cm. The fur is brown. The ears are much reduced in size and the eyes are near the top of the head. The feet are equipped with stout claws for burrowing and are fringed with bristles.

The tucotuco is colonial and lives in tunnels several yards long and about 30cm below the surface. Food is stored in chambers adjacent to the nesting area. **19d**

Pampas guinea pig   *Cavia pamparum*   RODENTIA
There are several species of guinea pig or cavy in South America and they occupy a wide variety of habitats. This species is found in the grasslands.

It has a round body, covered with reddish or grey-brown fur, short legs, rounded, naked ears and large eyes. It is 15–25cm long and weighs up to 0.9kg. It has no tail.

It lives in underground colonies. At dawn and dusk it feeds, in groups of 100 or more, taking grasses, tubers, leaves and fruit. 3–4 young are born after 66–72 days' gestation. **19e**

AFRICA

Yellow baboon   *(Papio cynocephalus)*   PRIMATES
This baboon lives in east and central Africa where it wanders about in large troops of up to 80 individuals, with males at the front and back and females and young in the middle.

The distinctive elongated muzzle with nostrils at the very tip of the snout has given rise to the name 'dog-faced monkey'. About the size of a large dog, the baboon is grizzled yellowish brown in colour, darker on the sides and back and blackish on the face. The buttocks are bare and calloused. The tail is a moderate length and bent downwards. As the arms and legs are about the same length, the baboon is better adapted for walking on all fours rather than upright.

It feeds mostly on fruit, roots and birds' eggs and may cause much damage in cultivated areas. **20a**

Sable antelope   *Hippotragus niger niger*   ARTIODACTYLA
This handsome antelope was originally found throughout southern and western Africa but its numbers are now much reduced. Normally found in herds of 20–30, it lives in bush country during the dry season, often descending to more thickly wooded parts during the rainy season.

It is 122–137cm high at the shoulder and, compared with the roan, the horns are longer (127cm) and more curved. The male has a velvety black coat with white on the under parts and sides of the face. The female is reddish brown. The mane is larger than in the roan. **20b**

Ratel   *Mellivora capensis*   CARNIVORA
The ratel or honey badger is found over most of Africa south of the Sahara, especially southern Africa, and also extends eastwards into Arabia and India.

Similar to a badger in appearance, the ratel is about 76cm long and about 25cm high at the shoulder. It has an ash grey back and dark blackish brown under parts. The legs are short and stout and the fore feet powerfully clawed for digging. The tail is about 25cm long.

The ratel emerges from its burrow at dusk to hunt for birds, rodents and insects and the honey of wild bees. The female generally gives birth to 2 young at a time. **20c**

Aardvark   *Orycteropus afer*   TUBULIDENTATA
The aardvark, ant bear or earth pig ranges from Ethiopia and Sudan southwards to the Cape.

The body is heavy and rather ungainly, about 183cm long, including a tail of 61cm, usually reddish grey in colour and sparsely covered with bristly hair. The head is elongated with a tubular, mobile snout and enormous pointed ears, rather like those of a hare. The back is arched and the tail is long, cylindrical and pointed. The hind feet have 5 toes, each with a claw, and there are strong claws on the fore feet with which it breaks open termite nests.

The tongue is 46cm long when extruded and coated with a sticky substance which enables the animal to pick up the termites on which it feeds. Nocturnal in habit, the aardvark lives in a burrow and the female gives birth to a single young in May—July. **20d**

Roan antelope   *Hippotragus equinus*   ARTIODACTYLA
This species lives in small herds of a dozen or so in open woodland and bush from western to eastern Africa.

It stands about 145cm at the shoulder and is greyish roan in colour with white under parts and face markings and some dark markings on the head. The stout horns, ringed for most of their length (up to 99cm), rise vertically from a ridge on the skull and curve boldly backwards. They are usually shorter in the female. The ears are very large and tufted and there is a small erect mane along the neck and shoulders. The tail is relatively short and tufted. **20e**

Cape buffalo   *Syncerus caffer*   ARTIODACTYLA
The Cape or African buffalo lives in herds of up to 1000 in most parts of Africa south of the Sahara Desert where water is available. It grazes at night and lies up in dense bush during the day.

This massive animal stands about 152cm at the shoulder and its great horns, with a span of up to 137cm, are much flattened at the base and curve outwards and downwards before sweeping up to a point. With increasing age, the bases of the horns in the bull almost meet in the middle, to form a sort of helmet. The head is relatively short with an expanded muzzle; the ears are large and the legs are short and stout. The tail is tufted at the tip. **20f**

African elephant   *Loxodonta africana*   PROBOSCIDEA
The elephant lives in herds over practically all of tropical Africa.

The largest living land animal, a fully grown male is up to 320cm high and weighs up to 6 tonnes. The African elephant is distinguished from the Indian by its enormous ears (which completely cover the shoulders and can be extended almost at right angles to the head when excited or when cooling itself), its convex forehead and the 2 finger-like protrusions at the tip of the trunk. The tusks can be up to 335cm long and correspond to the incisors of other mammals. A pair can weigh 63–72kg and hunting for this valuable ivory is now strictly controlled although there is still much poaching. The tail is long and round with a tuft of hair at the end.

The elephant feeds on grass, leaves, the bark of trees and fruits and can eat up to 90kg daily. **21a**

Gerenuk   *Litocranius walleri*   ARTIODACTYLA
The gerenuk or Waller's gazelle is to be found in the scattered bush country of east Africa.

It is fairly small, only 100cm high at the shoulder and 137cm long from nose to tail tip. However, by standing on its hind legs, and because of its very long thin neck, it can reach foliage up to 244cm from the ground. The male has horns about 38cm long, which curve backwards with a forward hook at the tip. Both sexes are chestnut in colour, with fawn flanks and white under parts.

It feeds mainly on acacia leaves. **21b**

Cape hunting dog   *Lycaon pictus*   CARNIVORA
Several local races of hunting dog occur south of the Sahara.

An odd-looking animal, it can be distinguished from other species of dog by having only 4 toes on each foot. It stands about 60cm high at the shoulder and is up to 107cm long with a tail of 38–40cm. The coat is an irregular patchwork of reddish yellow, black and white. The muzzle is dark, the tail has a bushy white tip and the ears are large and rounded.

It hunts in packs, preying on antelopes and any other game it can overpower. Up to 10 pups are born at a time, after a gestation period of about 2 months. **21c**

Grant's gazelle *Gazella granti* ARTIODACTYLA
This gazelle lives on the drier open plains of much of east Africa, from Ethiopia and Somaliland as far south as Tanzania, occasionally in herds of 50–100, and often in the company of zebras and gnus.

It stands about 76–84cm at the shoulder and is pale red-brown in colour above with white under parts and a white rump patch. There is a white streak down either side of the face and a darker stripe on the nose. The horns, which are found in both sexes, are long (62–76cm), curved, sub-lyrate and ringed throughout their length. They rise in a graceful sweep from the head, curving backwards and recurving at the tips. **21d**

Common eland *Taurotragus oryx oryx* ARTIODACTYLA
The eland lives, normally in herds, in bush and grassland in eastern Africa and as far south as the Cape.

The largest of the African antelopes, an adult male is up to 183cm high at the shoulder and up to 274cm long. The tail is up to 60cm long with a distinct tuft. The horns are spirally twisted and rise straight up in the plane of the face. Those of the female are slightly longer (99cm) than those of the male (94cm). The body is stout and heavily built and pale tawny grey in colour with white stripes down the sides. A pendulous dewlap hangs below the throat and the muzzle is naked.

The gestation period is 255–270 days and there is usually a single calf at a birth. **21e**

Kirk's dik-dik *Madoqua kirki* ARTIODACTYLA
There are several species of dik-dik, all very similar, except for size, and concentrated in east and south-west Africa. Kirk's dik-dik is found in east Africa and Namibia.

It is a small dainty animal about 30–36cm high at the shoulder with slender limbs. The face is long and the muzzle is elongated and slightly curved. Short ringed horns are found in the male.

The dik-dik lives alone, in pairs or in family groups, lying in thickets during the day and emerging at night to feed on leaves and shoots from the lowest branches and perhaps on some grass. The female bears a single young. **21f**

Impala *Aepyceros melampus* ARTIODACTYLA
The impala frequents open bush in southern and eastern Africa, where it lives in herds of 20–100.

It stands about 91cm high at the shoulder and weighs about 68kg. The sleek coat is dark reddish brown about and fawn merging into white below. There is also a white eyepatch and tip to the muzzle. The legs are long and slender with a black tuft on each fetlock and no lateral hooves. The male has lyrate, divergent horns, up to 76cm long, with up to 12 separate rings.

It relies on speed and its great leaping power to protect it from predators. **22a**

Spotted hyena *Crocuta crocuta* CARNIVORA
Found mainly in east Africa, this is the largest of the 3 species of hyena.

It stands about 76cm at the shoulder and is about 152cm long with a tail of a further 25cm. The fur is yellowish brown with darker brown spots which extend down the limbs. The hind legs are rather longer than the fore legs. The ears are smaller and more rounded than in the other species. The jaws are extremely powerful.

It feeds on carrion left by other predators but will also kill ungulates up to the size of a zebra. It will also attack domesticated animals. The young are born, 1–2 in number, after 110 days' gestation. **22b**

Grysbok *Raphicerus melanotis* ARTIODACTYLA
This small antelope lives either alone or in pairs over much of southern Africa as far north as the Zambesi, inhabiting hilly districts where there is plenty of cover.

It stands about 56cm high at the shoulder. The male has short horns about 9cm long. The ears are about twice this length. The coat is darkish brown, with scattered white hairs. The tail is shortish, the legs slender and the hooves are small and neat. **22c**

Giraffe *Giraffa camelopardis* ARTIODACTYLA
The giraffe ranges from Somalia and the Sudan to southern Africa and westwards to northern Nigeria, where it lives in open acacia savanna country.

It is the tallest mammal, with greatly elongated neck and limbs and a large body. The medium-sized tail is tipped with a large tuft of black hair. The elongated head has an elevated forehead with up to 5 short stubby horns, according to race. In the southern form, the hide is yellowish fawn with irregular brown patches on the body and upper legs. In the reticulated form, it is reddish brown with a network of fine yellow lines.

With its long protrusible tongue and prehensile upper lip, it browses on the leaves of acacia and thorn scrub. To drink, it straddles its legs in order to lower its head to the water. For defence, it relies on its hooves and its speed, which is considerable. **22d**

Hippopotamus   *Hippopotamus amphibius*   ARTIODACTYLA
This large ungainly animal is found over most of Africa south of the Sahara. It spends much of the day in water but emerges at night to feed on grasses and other plants.

It has a massive head set on a short thick neck, a stout, rounded body, very thick almost naked hide and short stout legs. It is 366–427cm long, standing 106–147cm at the shoulders and weighing up to 4 tonnes. The muzzle is greatly expanded laterally, with pig-like teeth; the canines are very large and curve backwards. The eyes are small and pig-like. The small rounded ears, like the nostrils, can be closed when submerged. The feet are 4-toed.

The female gives birth to a single young, which weighs about 27kg and can walk and swim within 5 minutes. **22e**

Rock hyrax   *Procavia capensis capensis*   HYRACOIDEA
The hyrax or dassie is found on rocky outcrops and slopes throughout Africa and is probably the closest living relative to the elephant.

It is similar to a guinea pig in shape and weighs about 3kg. The ears and snout are short; the legs are short and sturdy and the toes bear flattened hoof-like nails. The coarse fur is brown above and paler underneath. A small glandular area in the middle of the back is surrounded by erectile hairs and is important in scent-signalling.

The hyrax lives in colonies and feeds on grasses, leaves and bark. The young, 2–3 in a litter, are born in spring. **22f**

Klipspringer   *Oreotragus oreotragus*   ARTIODACTYLA
This active little antelope lives alone or in small parties, mainly in rocky or mountainous districts, in eastern or southern Africa. Its numbers have been much reduced by hunting.

It is about 50cm high at the shoulders. The coat is thick with bristly hairs and is brownish yellow in colour with paler under parts. The tail is short and the feet are extremely small. The ears are large in proportion to the body and have dark streaks inside. The male has short (15cm) horns which rise vertically from the head.

The gestation period is 214 days. **23a**

Black-backed jackal   *Canis mesomelas*   CARNIVORA
This is probably the most handsome of the African jackals and is found in the open veldt over much of eastern Africa from Somalia to the Cape.

About 36cm high at the shoulder, it is reddish brown in colour with a whitish belly and a black 'saddle' liberally streaked with silver. The sharply pointed muzzle is similar to that of the fox. The legs are comparatively short and the tail is long and bushy with a black tip.

At dusk and during the night, the jackal roams in pairs of family groups, searching for hares, rodents, ground-nesting birds and insects. It is also attracted to kills made by other predators. **23b**

Greater kudu   *Tragelephas strepsiceros*   ARTIODACTYLA
The kudu lives in small family groups in hilly country with plenty of cover in eastern Africa.

Handsomely marked, it stands about 152cm high at the shoulder. It is pale tawny or greyish brown in colour, with a white line down the centre of the back from which 5–8 vertical white stripes descend. The face has white markings. There is a mane on the neck and a fringe of longer hair on the throat. The male has large horns which rise in an open corkscrew spiral and are up to 122cm long.

It feeds mainly on leaves and young shoots. **23c**

Slender mongoose   *Herpestes sanguineus gracilis*   CARNIVORA
One of several African mongooses, this species is widely distributed south of the Sahara, where it lives on the ground, making its home in hollow trees, holes and empty burrows.

It resembles a large weasel, with a slender body, 30–35cm long, and long tail. Each hair of the fur is marked with light and dark rings which accounts for the grizzled greyish brown colour. The muzzle is short and pointed and the ears small and rounded. The tail is black-tipped and the legs are short. Each foot bears 5 toes.

It feeds on small mammals, reptiles – especially snakes and lizards, insects, birds' eggs and fruit. **23d**

Cape pangolin   *Manis temmincki*   PHOLIDOTA
The Cape, Temminck's or short-tailed pangolin is found from South Africa northwards through east Africa to Uganda and Kenya.

It is one of several African pangolins, all characterised by the absence of teeth and overlapping horny scales which cover the back, sides, tail and legs, and it can be distinguished by its blunt-tipped shorter tail. A fully grown specimen is up to 122cm long, including the tail, and weighs up to 18kg. It is greyish yellow-brown in colour. The legs are short and each foot has 5 clawed toes. The claws of the fore feet are the larger. The head is small and pointed.

As in the anteaters, the tongue is long and prehensile for collecting ants and termites. It is nocturnal, spending the day underground. It rolls itself up to form an armour-plated ball when attacked. **23e**

South African porcupine   *Hystrix africaeaustralis*   RODENTIA
The word porcupine comes from the French *porc épin* and this particular species is found in most of southern Africa, northwards to Tanzania.

Similar to a badger in size, this species is distinguished by the great length of the quills which are pointed at the tips and ringed with black and white. The quills are hollow and are erected when the animal is alarmed. They rattle when in motion. The body is brownish black with a white band at the base. The large erectile crest on the neck is blackish at the base, turning to white and the ears are tiny. The legs are short and there is a small thumb on each fore foot.

It is mainly solitary, living in holes or hollows during the day and emerging at night to feed on roots, maize and fruits. **23f**

Lion   *Panthera leo*   CARNIVORA
The lion occurs in many parts of Africa but its numbers are now reduced. It has become extinct in Asia and India, apart from a few in the Gir Forest Reserve.

A good-sized male is up to 275cm long, including the 90cm tail, and stands about 107cm at the shoulder. The long hairy mane and the long brush at the tip of the tail are characteristic. Both sexes are tawny brown although the cubs have a dark dorsal stripe and dark spots down the sides.

The lion lives in prides of 10–20 in open country with scattered bushes and reed beds. They cooperate in hunting their prey, mainly zebras and antelopes. The gestation period is 105–112 days, after which 2–5 cubs are born. These are blind for the first 6 days and are weaned at 3 months. **23g**

Vervet monkey   *Cercopithecus aethiops* var. *sabaeus*   PRIMATES
The vervet or green monkey is one of a group known as guenons. It lives mainly in open woodland and secondary bush in many parts of western, eastern and southern Africa.

The fur, due to the mixture of black and yellow hairs, is greenish.

1 **Polar regions: Arctic ice.** a) Ring seal. b) Polar bear. c) Atlantic walrus. d) Harp seal.

2 **Polar regions: Antarctic ice.** a) Ross seal. b) Weddell seal. c) Crabeater seal. d) Southern elephant seal.

3 **Polar regions: North American tundra.** a) Arctic souslik. b) Caribou. c) Musk ox. d) Wolf.

4 Polar regions: Eurasian tundra. a) Stoat. b) Arctic fox. c) Norwegian lemming. d) Varying hare.

5 **Coniferous forest: North America.** a) North American flying squirrel. b) Grizzly bear. c) Canada lynx. d) Marmot. e) Eastern chipmunk. f) American marten.

6 **Coniferous forest: North America.** a) Least weasel. b) Black bear. c) Canadian porcupine. d) Moose. e) Snowshoe rabbit. f) Canadian beaver.

7 **Coniferous forest: Eurasia.** a) Red squirrel. b) Pine marten. c) Wolverine. d) Brown bear. e) Common European shrew. f) Weasel.

8 Deciduous forest: North America. a) Common opossum. b) Grey squirrel. c) Wapiti. d) White-tailed deer. e) Bay lynx. f) North American raccoon. g) Striped skunk.

9 Deciduous forest: Eurasia. a) Hazel dormouse. b) Wild boar. c) Red deer. d) Black rat. e) European wild cat. f) Otter.

10 **Deciduous forest: Eurasia.** a) Pipistrelle bat. b) Eurasian badger. c) Roe deer. d) European hedgehog. e) Wood mouse. f) Red fox. g) European mole.

11 **Mediterranean scrub.** a) European polecat. b) Mouflon. c) Fallow deer. d) Rabbit. e) Mole-rat.

12 **Evergreen forest: Asia.** a) Red panda. b) Giant panda. c) Tahr. d) Chinese water deer. e) Chinese muntjac deer.

13 Evergreen forest: Australia. a) Sugar glider. b) Great glider. c) Eastern native cat. d) Dingo. e) Wombat. f) Rabbit bandicoot. g) Tasmanian devil.

14 **Evergreen forest: Australia.** a) Koala. b) Brush-tailed opossum. c) Banded numbat. d) Brush-tailed phascogale. e) Tasmanian wolf. f) Duck-billed playtypus.

15 Grasslands: North America. a) Spotted skunk. b) Pronghorn. c) American bison. d) Black-tailed prairie marmot. e) Coyote. f) American badger.

16 **Grasslands: Eurasia.** a) Brown hare. b) Water vole. c) European souslik. d) Common hamster. e) Saiga.

17 **Grasslands: Asia.** a) Persian lynx. b) Indian pangolin. c) Indian grey mongoose. d) Blackbuck. e) Nilgai. f) Cheetah.

18 Grasslands: South America. a) Pampas deer. b) Hairy armadillo. c) Maned wolf. d) Burmeister's fairy armadillo. e) Giant anteater.

19 Grasslands: South America. a) Mara. b) Pampas fox. c) Plains viscacha. d) Tucotuco. e) Pampas guinea pig.

20 Grasslands: Africa. a) Yellow baboon. b) Sable antelope. c) Ratel. d) Aardvark. e) Roan antelope. f) Cape buffalo.

21 Grasslands: Africa. a) African elephant. b) Gerenuk. c) Cape hunting dog. d) Grant's gazelle. e) Common eland. f) Dik dik.

22 **Grasslands: Africa.** a) Impala. b) Spotted hyena. c) Grysbok. d) Giraffe. e) Hippopotamus. f) Rock hyrax.

23 **Grasslands: Africa.** a) Klipspringer. b) Black-backed jackal. c) Greater kudu. d) Slender mongoose. e) Cape pangolin. f) South African porcupine. g) Lion.

24 **Grasslands: Africa.** a) Vervet monkey. b) Black rhinoceros. c) Sassaby. d) Nyala. e) Reedbuck. f) Yellow mongoose.

25 Grasslands: Africa. a) Wart hog. b) Common waterbuck. c) Steinbok. d) Blue wildebeeste. e) Serval.

26 Grasslands: Australia. a) Quokka. b) Crest-tailed marsupial mouse. c) Red kangaroo. d) Great grey kangaroo. e) Echidna.

27 Grasslands: Australia. a) Potaroo. b) Hare wallaby. c) Brush-tailed rock wallaby. d) Wallaroo. e) Red-necked wallaby. f) Hopping mouse.

28 Deserts: North America. a) Kit fox. b) Merriam's kangaroo rat. c) Black-tailed jack rabbit. d) Desert wood rat. e) Pocket mouse.

29 Deserts: Africa. a) Addax. b) Dorcas gazelle. c) Fennec fox. d) Arabian camel. e) Sand-dune cat. f) Springbok.

30 **Deserts: Eurasia.** a) Goitered gazelle. b) Bactrian camel. c) Egyptian jerboa. d) Long-eared hedgehog. e) Onager.

31 Tropical rain forest: Asia. a) Sun bear. b) Binturong. c) Banteng. d) Anoa. e) Water buffalo. f) Babirusa.

32 **Tropical rain forest: Asia.** a) Colugo. b) Golden cat. c) Musang. d) Indian chevrotain. e) Sambar deer. f) Axis deer.

33 Tropical rain forest: Asia. a) Lar gibbon. b) Greater Indian fruit bat. c) Leopard. d) Indian elephant. e) Entellus langur. f) Gaur.

34 **Tropical rain forest: Asia.** a) Rhesus monkey. b) Orang utan. c) Great crested porcupine. d) Clouded leopard. e) Spotted linsang. f) Slender loris.

35 Tropical rain forest: Asia. a) Malayan tapir. b) Indian palm squirrel. c) Celebes tarsier. d) Tiger. e) Indian rhinoceros. f) Moon rat.

36 Tropical rain forest: South America. a) Common vampire bat. b) Weeper capuchin. c) White-nosed coati. d) Capybara. e) Giant armadillo. f) Golden agouti.

37 **Tropical rain forest: South America.** a) Red-faced spider monkey. b) Kinkajou. c) Golden lion marmoset. d) Jaguar. e) Black-tailed marmoset. f) Red howler monkey.

38 **Tropical rain forest: South America.** a) Tamandua. b) Paca. c) Woolly opossum. d) Ocelot. e) White-lipped peccary. f) Two-toed sloth.

39 Tropical rain forest: Africa. a) Potto. b) Red colobus monkey. c) African brush-tailed porcupine. d) Small-scaled tree pangolin. e) Chequered elephant shrew. f) Okapi.

40 **Tropical rain forest: Africa.** a) Bushpig. b) African civet. c) Senegal bushbaby. d) Chimpanzee. e) Water chevrotain. f) Bushbuck.

41 Tropical rain forest: Africa. a) Mandrill. b) Gorilla. c) Black mangabey. d) Red duiker. e) Giant forest hog.

42 **Tropical rain forest: Malagasy Republic.** a) Ring-tailed mongoose. b) Aye aye. c) Ring-tailed lemur. d) Tenrec.

43 Tropical rain forest: Australia/New Guinea. a) Black tree kangaroo. b) New Guinea spotted cuscus. c) Spotted native cat. d) New Guinea anteater. e) Flying fox.

44 Mountains: North America. a) Puma. b) Alpine chipmunk. c) Rocky Mountain goat. d) Dall's sheep. e) Hoary marmot. f) Bighorn.

45 Mountains: Eurasia. a) Alpine marmot. b) Wild yak. c) Chamois. d) Snow leopard. e) Argali. f) Alpine ibex.

46 Mountains: South America. a) Chinchilla. b) Spectacled bear. c) Vicuna. d) Llama. e) Guanaco.

47 Mountains: Africa. a) Barbary sheep. b) Nubian ibex. c) Cape mountain zebra.

48 Oceans. a) Common dolphin. b) Sperm whale. c) Greenland right whale. d) Dugong. e) Californian sea-lion. f) Grey seal.

The throat, whiskers, under parts and the tip of the tail are more yellow. The face, hands and feet are blackish. Sometimes there is a narrow band of a paler shade over the eyes. **24a**

Black rhinoceros *Diceros bicornis* PERISSODACTYLA
There are two species of rhinoceros in Africa, the black and the white. The black rhinoceros, which is the more common, is found in dense bush over much of central and eastern Africa.

Both species have thick slaty grey hide but the black rhinoceros has a pointed prehensile upper lip, whereas the white rhinoceros has a blunt truncated muzzle. The black species is also slightly smaller, standing about 168cm at the shoulder, with an average maximum length of 365cm for a fully grown male. The 2 horns, which are composed of compressed keratin, lie in the mid-line of the forehead. The front horn is the larger, about 50cm long on average.

It feeds mainly on leaves, twigs and grass. Because of its poor eyesight it relies very much on scent. **24b**

Sassaby *Damaliscus lunatus* ARTIODACTYLA
The sassaby or bastard hartebeeste lives in herds on the grassy veldt of southern and south-eastern Africa and is said to be the fastest hoofed animal.

It stands about 122cm high at the shoulder and weighs up to 180kg. The body is deep and humped on the shoulder. The hide is a dark chestnut red with a black stripe down the centre of the head. The horns spread outwards from the base and then turn back and inwards. They are ringed near the head and rarely grow more than 38cm long. **24c**

Nyala *Tragelaphus angasi* ARTIODACTYLA
The nyala is one of the so-called harnessed antelopes. It lives in pairs or small family groups in south-eastern Africa.

The male is about 102cm high at the shoulder and is black and chestnut in colour with whitish stripes and spots on the flanks and long fringes of hair on the throat and belly. The female has a brighter chestnut coat with more strongly developed white stripes. The horns, which are only found in the male, are roughish on the surface and twisted, and are up to 84cm long. **24d**

Reedbuck *Redunca arundinum* ARTIODACTYLA
The reedbuck is found south of the Sahara in long grass on the hills and in valleys where water is plentiful. There are several local races

from the Transvaal to Angola and from Kenya.

An adult male is about 91cm high at the shoulder and the horns, which usually rise vertically in the plane of the head and bend forward at the tips, are 36–38cm long. The coat is reddish brown or greyish brown above, with whitish under parts, and becomes paler with age. The tail is short and bushy and the head is rather goat-like. It lives alone or in small groups. **24e**

Yellow mongoose   *Cynictis penicillata*   CARNIVORA
The yellow mongoose or meerkat lives in large colonies, each family occupying a burrow in the loose ground. It comes from the more southerly parts of Africa, particularly Cape Province, where it lives mainly in dry arid regions. There are local races, extending as far north as Tanzania, which differ slightly in colouration.

About 30cm long, with a large bushy tail of 20–23cm, it has yellowish brown fur, paler on the under parts, throat and edges of the rather small rounded ears. It is rather like an elongated squirrel.

It feeds mainly on small birds, their eggs, insects and small mammals. **24f**

Wart hog   *Phacochoerus aethiopicus*   ARTIODACTYLA
The wart hog lives in family parties in open bush from Ethiopia in the north, south to the Orange River and west to Senegal.

The head is enormous, relative to the body, with a flat broad warty muzzle and 2 upper tusks that curl upwards and inwards. The body is rounded and almost hairless, apart from the stiff mane on the back and neck. The tail is fairly long and tufted. The ears are small and pointed. A fully grown male may reach 152cm in length.

An omnivorous animal, the wart hog lives in burrows, often those abandoned by aardvarks. **25a**

Common waterbuck   *Kobus ellipsiprymnus*   ARTIODACTYLA
The waterbuck is found in open grassy or swampy country from western to eastern Africa, often in herds of up to 20 animals.

It stands about 122cm high at the shoulder and weighs up to 200kg. The shaggy coat is reddish brown with a white chevron at the throat, white eye streak and muzzle patch and white marks inside the ears. On the rump above the tail there is a narrow white ring, characteristic of this species. The male has horns up to 76cm long which sweep upwards and slightly backwards, and forward at the tips. They are prominently ringed. **25b**

Steinbok *Raphicerus campestris* ARTIODACTYLA
The steinbok lives alone or in pairs in the long grass of the open bush. It ranges from east to southern Africa.

It is a small antelope, weighing about 11kg and standing 50–56cm at the shoulder. The small upright horns of the male are up to 10cm long. The ears are erect and long in proportion to the head whilst the tail is very short.

Little is known of its breeding habits. The gestation period is 210 days. **25c**

Blue wildebeeste *Connochautes taurinus* ARTIODACTYLA
The blue wildebeeste or brindled gnu is found in herds on the grassy veldt of southern Africa and northwards to Tanzania and Kenya.

It stands about 122cm high at the shoulder. The head is like that of a buffalo, with broad horns, thick at the base, which curve outwards and then inwards and upwards. They are 62–76cm long and present in both male and female. The body is slaty roan with darker vertical stripes on the neck and shoulders. The long sad-looking face often has a whitish patch on each side under the eye. There is a thin pendant mane of black hair on the back and a dark fringe under the throat. The tail is long, black and tufted.

When fresh grass is unavailable the gnu may resort to wild melons and other supplementary foods. The female generally gives birth each year. **25d**

Serval *Felis serval* CARNIVORA
The serval is found in bush country in most parts of Africa south of the Sahara.

It is a medium-sized cat about 76cm long and 50cm high at the shoulder. The ears are very large. The tail is 23–25cm long with alternate black and yellow rings and tipped with black. The body is yellowish with bold black spotting and the legs are relatively long.

It is nocturnal, lying up during the day and hunting small animals, such as rodents and birds, as soon as darkness falls. The gestation period is 68–74 days. **25e**

AUSTRALIA

Quokka *Setonix brachyurus* MARSUPIALIA
This small scrub wallaby, also called the short-tailed pademelon, once roamed the coastal thickets and swamps of Western Australia, but is now confined to offshore islands in the south-west.

It is rather like a large rat, about 58cm long, stockily built, with a short tail only twice the length of its head. The feet are shorter than in other wallabies and the ears are very short. The fur is dark and grizzled. **26a**

Crest-tailed marsupial mouse *Sminthopsis crassicaudata* MARSUPIALIA
This small marsupial is found throughout central and southern Australia.

it is about the size of a field mouse, with a long, pointed nose, large eyes, large naked ears and a short, fat tail. It has 14 incisors compared the 4 of rodent mice.

It is diurnal and extremely aggressive, feeding on other marsupial mice, small rodents and insects. It nests beneath a log or stone. Up to 10 young are born and, after leaving the pouch, they cling to the mother's sides until able to fend for themselves. **26b**

Red kangaroo *Macropus rufus* MARSUPIALIA
This is the largest kangaroo and is found, in groups of 100 or so, on the central, western and eastern plains of Australia.

It is about 165cm tall with a tail about 107cm long. The short woolly fur of the body is generally rufous in the male and blue-grey in the female but this is by no means invariable.

It feeds mainly at dusk, remaining in the shade of bushes or trees during the heat of the day. It moves in a series of bounds, reaching a maximum speed of about 48km/h. The female produces a single young which is nurtured in the pouch. **26c**

Great grey kangaroo *Macropus major* MARSUPIALIA
The grey kangaroo is found in most of eastern Australia, with outlying populations in Tasmania and south-western Australia.

It is about 152cm high, with a tail of 90cm or so. The thick soft fur is greyish brown above and whitish on the belly. The tail is black-tipped. The head is small compared with the body, with a tapering muzzle and large, pointed ears, the fore feet are short with 5 toes but the hind feet are long and powerful with 4 toes. The tail acts as a prop when the animal sits and as a balancing organ when it is leaping.

The young is carried in the pouch of the female for 8 months after its birth. **26d**

Echidna *Tachyglossus aculeatus* MONOTREMATA
The echidna or Australian spiny anteater, like the duck-billed platypus, is an egg-laying mammal. It frequents rocky and sandy places where it constructs its burrow.

About 46–50cm long, with a vestigial tail, it is covered with stiff hairs and spines. The head is small and rounded with an elongated bare snout, with the nostrils at the end. The tongue is long and extensible for collecting ants. The short legs have feet with 5 strongly clawed toes; those of the hind feet are turned backward and outward when walking.

The female usually lays a single egg which is incubated in a fold on the underside of the body. Here the young remains throughout the suckling stage. **26e**

Potaroo *Potorous tridactylus* MARSUPIALIA
The potaroo or long-nosed kangaroo rat is found in New South Wales, Victoria, Tasmania and south-western Australia.

It is about 30cm long with a tail of about 20cm. The coat is dark greyish brown with an under fur generally of yellow. The belly is greyish white. The muzzle is rather elongated with naked skin on top. The ears are small and rounded and the tapering tail is prehensile at the tip. 2 of the 4 toes on each hind foot bear stout claws and all 5 toes of each fore foot are clawed.

It runs on all 4 feet but sits up on its hind feet, like a kangaroo, when stationary. It is nocturnal and feeds on root crops and grass, often damaging cultivated crops. **27a**

Hare wallaby *Lagorchestes leporoides* MARSUPIALIA
The hare wallaby lives on the plains of New South Wales and parts of South Australia but is now very rare.

It is similar to a hare in colour, size and general appearance. The body is about 50cm long and the tail, which has a few sparse hairs, is about 33cm long. The muzzle has hairs between the nostrils. The fore feet have 5 clawed toes and the hind feet have 4 toes. It is brown in colour with a yellowish grey belly.

The female produces a single young at a birth. **27b**

Brush-tailed rock wallaby *Petrogale penicillata* MARSUPIALIA
The rock wallabies form a distinct group among wallabies and are characterised by the naked end of the muzzle and the long bushy tail, which is comparatively thin and does not taper. The brush-tailed rock wallaby is found in dry forest areas fringing the plains, in eastern Queensland and New South Wales.

It is about 74cm long with a tail of 58cm or so. The back is grey-brown, the belly yellow-brown and there is a black marking in the armpit. **27c**

Wallaroo   *Macropus robustus*   MARSUPIALIA
The wallaroo, also known as the euro or hill kangaroo, is a close relation of the red and grey kangaroos but has become adapted for life in dry rocky areas on hillsides.

It is about 122cm tall and much sturdier than its cousins. Also the bare black patch around the nostrils is larger. There are no sweat glands but the wallaroo keeps cool by licking its forearms and allowing the moisture to evaporate. It can survive without water for 14 days or more. Its urine is very concentrated and it avoids high temperatures by sheltering in caves or under ledges during the day.

It feeds on succulent plants. **27d**

Red-necked wallaby   *Wallabia rufogrisea*   MARSUPIALIA
The red-necked or brush wallaby is found in dry open forest on the edge of the plains in eastern and south-eastern Australia. It is still fairly common, despite the demands of the fur trade.

Much smaller than the kangaroos, the red-necked wallaby is about 107cm high, with a powerful tail, about 76cm long, with a black tip. The fur is greyish to reddish fawn generally, rufous brown on the nape, shoulders and rump, and greyish white on the under parts.

A single young is born and is kept in the mother's pouch. **27e**

Hopping mouse   *Notomys mitchelli*   RODENTIA
Also known as the kangaroo mouse, because of the way it moves, this rodent is found on the dry plains of Australia.

It is a small mouse with large eyes and ears. The colour is generally brown with white under parts. The long tail is used for balance when it is moving at speed on its hind legs.

It leaves its burrow to feed at night on seeds, nuts and berries from which it obtains all its moisture. It does not need to drink and has highly concentrated urine. **27f**

5
Deserts

Desert conditions occur on the western margins of land masses, e.g. the deserts of Peru, of California, Arizona and Mexico, the Kalahari in South Africa, or in the interior, e.g. the Thar and Gobi Deserts of Eurasia, the Sahara of north Africa, which extends from coast to coast, and the desert areas of Western Australia.

The climate is characterised by low humidity and high evaporation. Rainfall is less than 25cm per annum and occurs as flash floods. The temperature fluctuates tremendously, from 48–54°C at mid-day to 15–21°C in the evening. Lack of water means lack of vegetation and, without dead leaves, roots, etc., it is very difficult for a soil to form. The substrate may consist of loose shifting sand, baked clay or bare rock surface covered with boulders. Vegetation is sparse and restricted to cactus, with wide-spreading shallow roots, tough wiry grasses or small thorn bushes with long tap roots. These plants experience brief periods of growth and blossom after the rains. There is little shade or shelter and objects can be seen from a great distance.

The demands of such an environment are as hazardous as those of the polar regions and, correspondingly, we find that the species of desert mammals are few in number and highly adapted. Apart from the camel and a few hooved mammals, most desert mammals are small, a factor which facilitates heat loss. It is, therefore, not surprising to find that rodents in particular have become adapted to desert conditions. However, other mammals, such as the sand-dune cat and the fennec fox, are notably smaller than their counterparts elsewhere. Colouration is generally a sandy brown for camouflage.

The ears in desert animals, e.g. those of the long-eared hedgehog, are large; in the case of the jack rabbit, they are also well supplied with blood vessels. Such ears serve not only to radiate heat but also, in an environment where there is little cover, to increase the sensitivity to sound. In some species, the internal ear is also modified. The eyes tend to be large. Elongated hind legs are common to many desert mammals and enable them to stand up and see a lot further. The long hind legs also permit rapid movement, so that much more territory can be covered in search of food, which is always scarce.

Large furry feet are another characteristic. Their size prevents the animal from sinking into the ground, by spreading its weight, and the fur provides protection from the heat. In sandy deserts, where there are frequent storms, the nostrils and ears, particularly of burrowing animals, often have protective bristles or tufts of hair. Eyelashes also tend to be long.

The larger animals tend to have more control over their body temperature – they both lose and absorb heat less quickly than the smaller creatures. The thick insulating coat of the camel helps in this respect whereas the red kangaroo of Australia reduces the problem of overheating by having reflective fur.

Physiologically, adaptations to conserve water are a common feature. The smaller mammals have no sweat glands and do not pant so they cannot cool themselves by evaporation. Red kangaroos and euros, however, cool themselves by spreading saliva over the exposed parts of their bodies and allowing it to evaporate. Generally, the kidneys secrete highly concentrated urine and water is removed from the faeces by specialised areas of the intestine. The euro of Australia does not excrete urine but recycles urea through its digestive tract. In the case of the herbivores, moisture is obtained from seeds and plant materials whereas the carnivores obtain it from their prey. Most animals can do without water for a considerable period. Water is also obtained by the metabolism of carbohydrates; the camel utilises the fat in its hump whereas the gerbil makes use of the carbohydrates in the seeds which it eats. The onager and the camel can both withstand a loss of 30 and 40% of their body water respectively (compared with 20% for other mammals) and the camel does not begin to sweat until its body temperature reaches 41°C (cf. 37°C).

Behavioural characteristics are also important in survival. Burrowing not only provides protection from temperature extremes (a constant 30°C is found 1m below the desert surface) but also conserves water.

NORTH AMERICA

Kit fox   *Vulpes velox*   CARNIVORA

The kit fox occurs as a northern and southern form in arid regions of the western USA. The southern form, which had become very rare, is now re-establishing itself.

It is a well built animal, standing about 30cm high at the shoulder and 90cm long overall. It weighs 1.8–2.3kg. The coat is yellowish brown and speckled with silvery black-tipped guard hairs. The bushy tail is also tipped with black. Like the fennec fox of Africa, the ears are large, erect and pointed and serve to radiate heat.

It is nocturnal, burrowing up to 1.5m below the surface to avoid the high daytime temperatures. Small rodents, birds, lizards and insects form the diet. Adults pair for a year or more and 4–5 cubs are born in the spring. **28a**

Merriam's kangaroo rat *Dipodomys merriami* RODENTIA
The kangaroo rat is found in arid areas of Mexico and the western USA.

It has a stocky body about 10cm long and a hairy tail of about 15cm, with a bushy tip. The fur is brownish above with dark-tipped guard hairs and paler on the under side. The short front legs are used for burrowing and the very long back legs enable the animal to hop like a kangaroo. The tail is used for balance when travelling and as a prop when stationary. The ears are small but the eyes and whiskers are large for better perception at night. The urine is concentrated and there are no sweat glands.

The kangaroo rat does not drink but gets all its moisture from seeds and juicy tubers. **28b**

Black-tailed jack rabbit *Lepus californicus* LAGOMORPHA
Although commonly known as a rabbit, this animal is a true hare. It is found in the western USA, from Washington and South Dakota to Mexico.

It is pale brown in colour with black markings and black tips on its ears. The tail has a wide black stripe which runs on to the back. The hind legs are well developed and the hare can leap for 4m or more. The ears are broad and long and well supplied with blood vessels; these help to control body temperature by radiating excess heat.

The hare is active during the day, feeding on shoots, twigs, bark, leaves and buds. 3–4 litters of 1–6 young are produced each year. **28c**

Desert wood rat *Neotoma lepida* RODENTIA
This species of wood rat is found in the deserts of Arizona.

It is about the size of a house rat. The fur is soft, greyish cinnamon-coloured on the back and white underneath. The eyes and ears are large and the whiskers are very long.

It is nocturnal and feeds on cactus, seeds, nuts and fruit, which are its only source of moisture. It lives in colonies but has its own nest of twigs, debris and cactus spines. There are 2 litters a year, of 2–6 young, which are born after 4 weeks' gestation. **28d**

Pocket mouse *Perognathus penicillatus* RODENTIA
This tiny mouse is found in western Canada and the USA, south to Central America.

It is about 7.5cm long with a furry, tufted tail of the same length. The fur is soft and buff in colour. The cheeks have fur-lined pockets which open to the outside and are used for transporting food. Its legs are all about the same length and it moves on all fours, sifting seeds from the sand with its long claws.

It avoids temperature extremes by burrowing, emerging at night to feed. 2–8 young are born after 4 weeks' gestation and there are generally 2 litters a year. **28e**

AFRICA

Addax *Addax nasomaculatus* ARTIODACTYLA
The addax is an endangered species and is found only sporadically across the southern Sahara from Mauretania in the west to the Sudan in the east.

It has a thickset body, about 107cm high at the shoulder, and shortish legs. The female is slightly smaller. Both sexes have horns but the male has up to 3 spirals compared with the 2 of the female. The coat is greyish white, sometimes tinged with russet, and the legs, hindquarters and under parts are white. The neck and shoulders are also ringed with chestnut, there is a distinctive white facial mark and the lips are white. The coat becomes darker and longer in the winter.

The addax rests during the day, and feeds at night on succulents and other desert plants. **29a**

Dorcas gazelle *Gazella dorcas* ARTIODACTYLA
This small gazelle is found in the deserts and arid plains of north Africa and Arabia.

It stands about 56cm high at the shoulder and has horns up to 33cm long. The reddish brown upper parts are separated from the sandy white under side by a dark stripe on the flank.

It feeds on grass when available and on succulent roots and plants. Depending on the season, it can go without water for 5–12 days. Speeds of 64–80km/h can be reached by this gazelle. **29b**

Fennec fox *Fennecus zerda* CARNIVORA
The fennec occurs throughout the deserts of north Africa and Arabia and shows many similarities to the kit fox of North America.

It is fairly small, about 40cm long with a tail of 30cm. The coat is fluffy and cream in colour and the bushy tail is used to protect the head from the sun. The tip of the nose is black and the eyes are large. The huge ears radiate heat during the day and can pick up sound well at night. The paws are large and furry, for digging and for protection from the hot sand.

The fennec can burrow very rapidly to escape from the sun. At night it hunts for insects, lizards, birds and small rodents which it stores under ground. It drinks when possible but also gets a lot of moisture from its prey. **29c**

Arabian camel   *Camelus dromedarius*   ARTIODACTYLA

In its wild state, this camel occurred in Arabia and on the borders of the Sahara, but it has been domesticated almost completely and now can be found in South Africa, Australia and southern Asia as well.

It is a large animal, standing 180–213cm high. The single hump distinguishes it from the bactrian camel. Also, the legs are longer and more slender and the feet are broader and flatter. The hair is fine and soft, generally sandy in colour but sometimes brown or black. The eyes are large, with long lashes, and the nostrils can be closed to exclude sand. To conserve water, the camel excretes concentrated urine and does not sweat until its body temperature reaches 41°C. It can also drink enormous quantities of water without harm because of modification of the blood.

It breeds every 2 years, giving birth to 1 offspring after 12 months' gestation. **29d**

Sand-dune cat   *Felis margarita*   CARNIVORA

The sand-dune cat is found in the Sahara and Arabia, where it lives in areas of constantly moving sand, and also in western Asia, where the sand is held together by desert plants, such as acacia.

It is a small cat, about 25cm high, with a long thickly furred tail. The face is flattish, with long sensitive whiskers. The ears, which are large and triangular, can be flattened completely. The feet have thickly padded soles for easier movement on the sand and for protection from the heat. The fur is sandy in colour with subtle red-brown stripes on the flanks and a scattering of dark hairs on the back and on the tail tip.

During the day it rests under vegetation or in a shallow burrow. It eats rodents, reptiles, birds and insects from which it appears to get sufficient liquid to do without water for long periods. **29e**

Springbok   *Antidorcas marsupialis*   ARTIODACTYLA
Although the springbok is the emblem of South Africa, the herds there are now very much reduced. However, it is still fairly common in more northerly areas, such as Angola, Botswana and the Kalahari, where it lives in open plain country bordering the desert.

It stands about 76cm high at the shoulder and the horns, which are found in both male and female, are black and lyrate, up to 38cm long and ringed for most of their length. The body is reddish fawn above with pale under parts separated by a dark band on each side. There is a lot of white on the face with a dark patch below the horns. The white crest in the middle of the lower back is erected when the animal is excited.

The name derives from its habit of leaping 2.5–3m into the air, with the legs held quite stiff, before taking flight. **29f**

Goitered gazelle   *Gazella subgutturosa*   ARTIODACTYLA
This gazelle occurs widely in the cold deserts of central Asia, extending westward into Iran.

It is fairly large, sandy brown above and white below, with a darker dividing streak on the flank. There is a conspicuous white rump and the under side of the tail is black. The lyrate horns are ridged and are generally absent in the female.

The gazelle lives in herds. A goitre-like swelling of the throat develops in the male when the breeding season starts. 2–3 young are born in the spring. **30a**

Bactrian camel   *Camelus bactrianus*   ARTIODACTYLA
A native of central Asia, from the Taurus to Manchuria, this camel is still found wild in Mongolia, although only in small numbers, and it has been much domesticated.

It is distinguished by its 2 humps. The reddish brown hair varies in shade from red to dark brown and is paler in the summer. The coat is thick and shaggy, especially on the head, neck, shoulders and humps, and on the front of the chest.

Compared with the Arabian camel, the stout legs are shorter and terminate in shorter and harder feet, better adapted to the exposed country where it lives. It feeds mainly on scrub and other steppe vegetation. The gestation period is about 13 months and normally only 1 offspring is born at a time. **30b**

Egyptian jerboa   *Jaculus jaculus*   RODENTIA
The jerboa lives in the sandy deserts of south-western Asia and is also

found in north Africa.

The fur is sandy in colour with white under parts. The tail is whitish underneath and has a bushy tip of black and white. About 16.5cm long, the jerboa has characteristic elongated hind legs and a tail generally longer than the body. The head is mouse-like with comparatively large eyes and ears. The small fore legs are held close to the chest when moving and are used mainly for handling food. The hind legs can move independently but the jerboa generally leaps about.

It spends the day in a hole, emerging at night to feed on seeds, and can go without water for long periods. **30c**

Long-eared hedgehog *Hemiechinus auritus* INSECTIVORA
This hedgehog lives in the desert areas of north Africa and the Middle East, ranging into south-west Asia.

The body is compact and slightly smaller than that of the European hedgehog and the protective spines are lighter in colour. The face, legs and under side are covered with soft pale fur. The legs are long and not only lift the body clear of the hot ground but also enable the hedgehog to run at comparatively great speeds when chasing prey. The long ears radiate heat to promote cooling as well as increasing sensitivity to sound.

The hedgehog avoids the heat of the day by retiring to its burrow and emerges at night to feed on insects, toads and small mammals. It seldom drinks but obtains all the moisture it needs from its prey. **30d**

Onager *Equus hemionus onager* PERIRSSODACTYLA
The onager or Persian wild ass lives in western central Asia and north-west India and extends westward into Iran, Baluchistan and Syria.

It stands about 107–114cm at the withers. The upper parts are fawny white with a blackish dorsal stripe, mane and tail tuft. The under parts are white. There is usually a yellowish patch on the flanks and the ears have black tips. The ears are shorter and narrower than in the grey wild asses of Africa.

The onager lives in herds which are led by an old experienced stallion. A single offspring is born after a gestation period of about 1 year. **30e**

6
Tropical rain forest

Tropical rain forest or *selvas* occurs on either side of the Equator between the Tropics of Cancer and Capricorn. It is found in the extreme south of North America, extending through Central America into the north-west of South America and the Amazon Basin, in the western half of equatorial Africa and the eastern Malagasy Republic, and throughout the Indo-Malayan archipelago into the north-west tip of Australia.

The climate in these regions is characterised by its consistency. The average annual temperature of 27°C is constant to within 2°C. Of the 200cm annual rainfall, no less than 12cm falls in any one month and, moreover, it rains every day. Humidity is high and constant, and day and night are of almost equal length.

Decay is rapid in such a climate and little humus gets into the soil. The heavy rains leach out what nutrients there are, leaving a poor, reddish soil known as *laterite*.

The forest itself is more luxuriant and more diverse in species than any other plant community. Both evergreen and deciduous trees occur – laurels, legumes, myrtles, mahogany, satinwood, but with no seasonal influence to affect growth patterns a large proportion of the latter is always in leaf. The trees are generally tall and slender, supported by buttress roots and branching near to the crown.

The forest falls naturally into layers. The majority of trees are between 45m and 55m high and their branches form the *canopy*. A few, even taller (up to 80m) *emergent* trees stand above the canopy. Not much light can penetrate this topmost layer and so the middle layers consist of smaller shade-loving trees and bushes, shrubs, giant ferns and palms. Except where a fallen tree allows the light to penetrate, the lowest level, the forest floor, supports only saprophytic fungi, which are independent of light. In order to reach the light many plants adopt a climbing habit, using established trees for support. Others have become *epiphytic*, attaching themselves to other plants but relying on the air, water and accumulated debris for nourishment.

The animal community is equally rich and diverse in species. The canopy is a rich source of fruit, flowers and buds and the Primates are probably the most well adapted of mammals for exploiting this food source. Some, e.g. the orang utan and spider monkey, move from branch to branch suspended by their long arms, a process known as *brachiation*, and others, such as the colobus monkey and the tarsier, can leap prodigious distances. Nearly all have opposable thumbs and big toes for grasping the branches and the South American species also have prehensile tails. Binocular and colour vision are important for judging distance and gathering food. Pangolins, anteaters, and sometimes rats, lemurs and shrews, are also found at this level, walking along the upper sides of the branches.

Some mammals have evolved membranes for gliding, as in the colugo, or flying, as in the bats. These tend to live in the middle levels of the forest where the foliage is not so dense. Many mammals at this level feed on either insects or fruit, e.g. the tamandua, sun bear, tree kangaroo and bushbaby, but a few carnivores are also found, such as the clouded leopard and the ocelot. Some carnivores, particularly the linsang and civets, make excursions into the trees from the forest floor in search of prey.

On the forest floor itself, the only plant food available is in the form of fungi, roots, bulbs, low bushes and decaying matter from the upper stories but there is a rich supply of insects for species such as the giant anteater, tenrec and moon rat. There are a few hooved mammals and, on the whole, these tend to be smaller than their grassland counterparts, e.g. the anoa, chevrotain and Indian elephant. Also their heads tend to be smaller and more pointed and horns and antlers are either absent or much reduced in size. These factors make movement though the undergrowth easier. Apart from the browsers, there are the scavengers, the small rodents with their omnivorous eating habits and the babirusa, peccary and porcupine, which root up bulbs and tubers from the soil. Carnivores are few as always and include such species as the golden cat, coati, civets, linsang and galidia.

ASIA

Sun bear   *Helarctos malayanus*   CARNIVORA
The sun or Malayan bear is the smallest of the bears and lives in South-East Asia, particularly Burma, Peninsular Malaysia, Thailand, Borneo and Sumatra.

It is 114–137cm long and stands only 60cm or so at the shoulders. Rather slender in build, with a short broad head and small well rounded ears, it is black in colour with a whitish or yellowish curved patch on the chest and a patch of similar colour on the snout. The limbs are relatively long and each foot has 5 toes, each with a long, curved non-retractile claw. The tongue is long for obtaining the wild honey to which this species is very partial.

It is a good climber and, apart from honey, feeds on fruits and insects. **31a**

Binturong   *Arctictis binturong*   CARNIVORA

The binturong is the largest member of the civet family and is widely distributed throughout South-East Asia.

Rather cat-like in appearance, it is about 76cm long with a tail of a further 60–68cm. The body hair is long and shaggy, black in colour with a sprinkling of white. Like the sloth, the presence of algae often gives it a greenish hue. The ears are tufted and the whiskers are long. The tail, which is prehensile, is strong and bushy. The teeth are blunt and small.

The binturong is arboreal and generally nocturnal in habit. Fruit is the staple diet but eggs and fledglings may also be eaten. **31b**

Banteng   *Bos javanicus*   ARTIODACTYLA

This wild ox is native to the forests of Borneo and Java.

It is very similar to the gaur. The adult male is solidly and powerfully built, standing over 180cm high at the shoulder. It is a glossy black in colour, with white socks, and can be distinguished from the gaur by the white rump patch. The horns are thick and curved. The cows and calves are a uniform reddish brown.

The banteng spends the day in the forest, coming out at night to graze on the river banks. **31c**

Anoa   *Anoa depressicornis*   ARTIODACTYLA

The anoa is also known as the dwarf buffalo or wood ox and is the smallest species of wild cattle. It is found on the island of Sulawesi (Celebes).

It is a sturdy creature with a stout body and short legs. The male is 101cm high at the shoulder and about 137cm long, with a tail of a further 30cm. The horns are about 30cm long and depressed backwards. Unusually in cattle, the broad muzzle is moist and naked. In the young, the coat is woolly and yellowish in colour, becoming smoother and changing to dark brown or black with age.

The anoa lives in pairs near water in upland forest, feeding largely on sugar cane and other crops. The young are born after 295 days' gestation. **31d**

Water buffalo *Bubalus bubalis* ARTIODACTYLA
This animal naturally lives in marsh or swampy areas and has been readily domesticated for such purposes as ploughing paddy fields, carrying loads and providing milk.

It stands 152–168cm high. The tail is about 91cm long, with a terminal tuft and the horns have a span of 183–244cm. Compared with the African buffalo, the head is longer, with a straighter profile, and the ears are smaller. The horns are long and flattened, with transverse wrinkles, and curve upwards and backwards from the head; the tips are bent forwards and inwards. The hide is greyish black in colour and becomes almost hairless with age. On the back, the hair along the mid-line is directed forwards, not backwards as in the African species. **31e**

Babirusa *Babirussa babirussa* ARTIODACTYLA
This wild pig, notable for its great upturned tusks, is found in the dense jungles of Sulawesi (Celebes).

Its stout body is covered in almost hairless, rough grey hide. The male has pairs of tusks which develop from the canine teeth. Those in the upper jaw grow upwards, through the skin of the face, and curve backwards almost to touch the forehead.

The babirusa is nocturnal in habit and feeds on plant and animal matter which it roots up from the soft soil near rivers and swamps. It lives in small family groups. **31f**

Colugo *Cynocephalus volans* DERMOPTERA
The colugo or flying lemur is a taxonomic puzzle, as the head shows features of both lemurs and insectivores. There are only 2 species in the order: one is found in Peninsular Malaysia, Borneo and Sumatra and the other is restricted to the Philippines.

The body is about 41cm long, with a tail of a further 28cm, and is covered with woolly fur. 'Wings' of skin stretch between the fore and hind limbs and extend to the shoulders. The colugo is a far more efficient glider than the flying squirrels or phalangers and seldom leaves the trees.

During the day it hangs from branches by its long claws with its head up. At night it feeds on young leaves, buds and fruit. **32a**

Golden cat *Felis temmincki* CARNIVORA
The golden cat ranges from Nepal and Assam to western China and south through Peninsular Malaysia to Sumatra.

It is about 81cm long with a tail of 43cm. The body is a plain rich golden brown. The under side is paler with black markings and the head is marked with white, black and grey stripes. The ears are very mobile and it has exceptional sight.

It feeds on rodents, pheasants and small deer. The female usually bears 2 young. **32b**

Musang   *Paradoxurus hermaphroditus*   CARNIVORA

The musang, common palm civet or toddy cat is found in India, Sri Lanka, western Malaysia, the Philippines and Indonesia.

The body is about 60cm long, with a tail of similar length. The legs are short, with 5 toes on the front feet, and the snout is pointed. The animal weighs 2.7–4.5kg. The long, coarse fur is blackish brown in colour with darker markings.

It feeds on fruit, birds, small mammals, amphibians and insects. There are 3–4 young to a litter. **32c**

Indian chevrotain   *Tragulus meminna*   ARTIODACTYLA

This timid forest dweller is one of the smallest of the hoofed animals. It is also known as the mouse deer and is similar in shape and size to the South American agouti and occupies a similar ecological niche.

It stands about 30cm high at the shoulder and weighs 2.7–4.5kg. The head is narrow and the muzzle pointed. Neither sex has horns or antlers but the male has long protruding upper canines. The coat is brown with paler spots and dashes and pale under parts. The young, 1–2 in number, are born after 120 days' gestation. **32d**

Sambar deer   *Cervus unicolor*   ARTIODACTYLA

The sambar inhabits well-wooded areas of India and Sri Lanka (Ceylon) and its range extends into South-East Asia.

This large deer stands about 152cm high at the shoulder. Its 3-tined antlers are up to 122cm long with a span of up to 96cm. The brow line forms a characteristic acute angle with the beam. The coat is dark brown, paler on the under parts, and the coarse wiry hair, which is also longer on the neck and throat, forms an erectile mane. The tail is small and thick.

Nocturnal in habit, it is seldom found in large numbers. There is usually 1 fawn at a birth. **32e**

Axis deer   *Axis axis*   ARTIODACTYLA

The axis or chital deer is found in forest regions and jungles of southern Asia and Sri Lanka (Ceylon).

The adult is approximately 150cm long, with a tail of a further 14–20cm, and stands 96cm at the shoulder. The coat is reddish or yellowish brown above with rows of white spots. The under parts and throat are white. The male has antlers with no more than 3 long, pointed tines.

It is active both by day and night, feeding on tree bark, young shoots and green leaves. Usually only 1 calf is born after 231–238 days' gestation. The females and young form herds. **32f**

Lar gibbon *Hylobates lar* PRIMATES
The lar or white-handed gibbon lives in the forests of Peninsular Malaysia, Thailand, Sumatra and Cambodia, where it spends most of its time in the trees. The long slender limbs are perfectly adapted for rapid progress from branch to branch and the feet are often used to carry food — fruit, young shoots and leaves. The gibbon is also truly bipedal and can walk in an upright position.

It is 76–91cm long and has no tail. The general body colour varies from greyish to yellowish brown, often paler on the back. The hands and feet are pale or whitish and the black face is framed with white hairs. It lives in troops of 6–20 and births are usually single. **33a**

Greater Indian fruit bat *Pteropus giganteus* CHIROPTERA
This is one of the largest and best known of the fruit bats. It is also known as the flying fox because of the appearance of the head. It is found in most of India, Sri Lanka (Ceylon) and Burma.

The body is 30cm or more in length and is covered in thick woolly fur. It is dark brown on the upper back, blackish brown on the ears, face and wings, and reddish brown elsewhere. The wings, with a span of up to 150cm, have 3 joints in the index finger and a claw on the tip of the second finger. (Other bats have a thumb-claw.)

During the day, it roosts in large flocks, emerging at dusk to search for fruit. **33b**

Leopard *Panthera pardus* CARNIVORA
The leopard is found in both Asia and Africa. Although smaller than the lion, it is just as dangerous, for it can climb trees and drop on its victims.

An adult is up to 213cm long, including a tail of 76–91cm, and stands about 60cm high at the shoulders. The fur is generally a deep yellow in colour, with dark spots or rosettes, and the under parts are white. Melanism is not uncommon and the black panther is in fact a melanistic leopard. The spots are somewhat smaller on the head and larger on the tail.

Nocturnal in habit, the leopard often raids villages for cattle and goats and it will store half-eaten carcasses in the trees. Cubs are usually born in the spring, 1–3 in number, after a gestation period of 90–95 days. **33c**

Indian elephant *Elephas maximus* PROBOSCIDEA
In the wild state, this elephant is found in forest regions of India, Sri Lanka (Ceylon), Burma, Thailand, Peninsula Malaysia and Sumatra, living in herds, usually close to water. In its domesticated form it is widely used for heavy haulage work and also in ceremonial processions.

Compared with the African species, it is smaller – a bull is 244–305cm high–the head is more dome-shaped and the ears are smaller. The tusks are only large in the bulls but rarely exceed 152–183cm. The hide is generally slate-grey and almost naked, with long hair on the tail only. The relatively smooth trunk is regularly tapered and ends in a single finger-like tip.

The female usually bears 1 calf after 21 months' gestation. **33d**

Entellus langur *Presbytis entellus* PRIMATES
The entellus langur or Hanuman monkey lives in large troops over much of India. Originally a forest-dweller, it now also frequents towns and villages.

Of all the langurs, or leaf monkeys, the entellus is easily distinguished because its tail is longer than its body. A fully grown specimen may be up to 76cm long with a tail, which is tufted, of up to 96cm. It is greyish brown in colour, except for the hands, face and feet, which are black. The hair radiates in all directions from a point on the forehead and projects over the eyes like the eaves of a house. The limbs are long and slender and the hands have well developed thumbs. The hind legs are the longer. **33e**

Gaur *Bos gaurus* ARTIODACTYLA
The gaur or seladang lives in upland forests of much of India and eastwards into Burma and Peninsula Malaysia. It travels in family parties or small herds.

It is powerfully and massively built with a conspicuous dorsal hump. An adult bull may stand up to 163cm at the shoulder. The distinctive horns curve throughout their length, bend backwards and inwards at the tips, and are flattened at the base. They are greenish in colour, grading to black at the tips, and are up to 86cm long. The colour of the hide is dark brown to blackish generally with paler under parts, and the lower legs are white. The tail is shortish and the

ears are large and pointed.
The cow usually gives birth to a single calf. **33f**

Rhesus monkey   *Macaca mulatta*   PRIMATES
The rhesus monkey ranges over much of northern India, including Kashmir and the foot-hills of the Himalayas, eastwards into Assam, Burma and China. It lives in large troops, frequently in or near towns and villages.

It belongs to the group of monkeys known as macaques, characterised by a long muzzle and large flesh-coloured naked buttocks. The body is about 60cm long, with a tail of about 25cm, and the fur is brownish tinged with grey or green. The face is bare and reddish in adults but paler in youngsters. It is fond of water and can swim quite well. **34a**

Orangutan   *Pongo pygmaeus*   PRIMATES
The orangutan is the largest anthropoid ape in Asia. It lives, alone or with a mate, in the dense forests of Borneo and Sumatra and is completely arboreal, its long arms being well adapted for swinging from branch to branch.

A fully grown male is about 137cm high and weighs about 90kg. Its arms are so long that the hands brush the ground as it walks. The skull rises into a pointed crown with only slight ridges over the eyes. The body is covered with long reddish brown hair and the face is bare and yellowish brown, becoming greyish with increasing age. The adult male usually has a fringe of hair around the face and a beard, while folds of skin around the neck form a collar. The legs are short and bowed with the knees turned out and the feet in.

It feeds mainly on fruit and the buds of plants. **34b**

Great crested porcupine   *Hystrix cristata*   RODENTIA
This porcupine is found in north and west Africa, Italy and Sicily and its range extends to south-west Asia.

The largest of the porcupines, it is over 91cm long and weighs 18–27kg. The body is thick-set, the legs are short and the quills are long and sharp.

It does not climb but makes extensive burrows which may be shared by several other porcupines. It feeds at dawn and dusk on bulbs, roots, bark and fallen fruit. **34c**

Clouded leopard   *Neofelis nebulosa*   CARNIVORA
The clouded leopard is purely arboreal in habit and is found from

southern China and Nepal, southwards to Peninsular Malaysia and Borneo.

It is 91–106cm long with a tail up to 91cm long. The body is slender with comparatively short legs and the head is longer in proportion to the body than that of most cats. The upper canines are particularly long. The fur is greyish brown or yellowish brown, with large dark blotches and streaks on the neck, back and limbs. There are also black stripes on the face, one just above the mouth and the other running from behind the eyes, past the ears to the neck. The tail often has more or less complete dark rings.

It feeds mainly on small birds and mammals, including some deer, monkeys and wild pigs. **34d**

Spotted linsang   *Prionodon pardicolor*   CARNIVORA
The linsang is a type of civet and typical of the small carnivores of tropical forests. It is found throughout India, Borneo and Sumatra and to the north-east into China.

It is long-bodied with short legs, a pointed snout and rounded ears. At the base of the long tail there are scent glands. The fur is soft and sandy in colour with dark blotches on the back and bands on the tail. The eyes are large.

The linsang spends the day in its den in the ground or in hollow trees. It lives alone or in pairs and there are 2–3 young in a litter. **34e**

Slender loris   *Loris tardigradus*   PRIMATES
The slender loris lives in southern India and Sri Lanka (Ceylon). It is a relative of the lemurs, from which it is distinguished by the very small index finger of the hand.

It is 20–25cm long, with long slender limbs, large close-set eyes, as befits a nocturnal mammal, and small ears which are partly buried in the fur. In both the hands and feet, the first digit diverges widely from the rest. The big toe appears almost to face backwards. The fur is darkish grey with a reddish tinge on the back and parts of the limbs and lighter under parts. A narrow white stripe is set vertically between the eyes and sometimes extends onto the forehead.

The loris feeds on fruit, insects, small birds and birds' eggs and sometimes the young shoots of trees. **34f**

Malayan tapir   *Tapirus indicus*   PERISSODACTYLA
This shy animal is found in the jungles of Peninsular Malaysia, southern Thailand and Sumatra, usually near water.

It is up to 244cm long, from the tip of the snout to the tail root, and stands about 107cm at the shoulder. The body is stoutly built with relatively short legs and the head is narrow. The muzzle terminates in a short trunk with large nostrils. The eyes are small and the ears are erect and oval in shape. The front part of the body and all 4 legs are blackish brown but from behind the fore legs to the upper thighs is white.

The tapir is nocturnal, feeding at night on vegetation. Usually a single offspring is born, which, for 4–6 months, is brownish black with spots and stripes of yellow on the sides and whitish on the under parts. **35a**

Indian palm squirrel   *Funambulus rufa*   RODENTIA
The palm squirrels are common throughout South-East Asia and this particular species occurs in India and Sri Lanka (Ceylon).

It is smaller than the northern squirrels and the tail is shorter and less bushy. The ears are not tufted. The fur is generally a mottled brown colour, paler on the head and under parts and with 5 distinctive stripes of white and russet on the back, from neck to tail.

It tends to move about in small groups on the ground, with frequent excursions into the lower and middle layers of the forest. It feeds mainly on vegetation but will also take small insects. **35b**

Celebes tarsier   *Tarsius spectrum*   PRIMATES
This tarsier is found in the shrubby layers of the jungle in Sulawesi (Celebes) and the surrounding islands.

It is about 15cm long with a long tail of 28cm which is naked and scaly on the under side. The tail is used for balance and as a brake. The head is round, with large naked bat-like ears and enormous eyes, and can be turned through 180°. The tips of the fingers and toes are expanded into sucker-like discs which enable the tarsier to grip the branches. The ankle bones are greatly elongated. It is nocturnal, feeding on insects and other small animals.

It lives singly or in pairs and feeds on insects, small birds and lizards and can leap great distances. It breeds all the year round and a single young is born after 6 months' gestation. **35c**

Tiger   *Panthera tigris*   CARNIVORA
This is the largest cat found in Asia and local races occur from Siberia and Mongolia in the north to India and Peninsular Malaysia in the south.

A fully grown male is 274–290cm long and weighs about 180–227kg. The female is about 30cm shorter and weighs 45kg less. The reddish fawn upper parts have black or blackish brown stripes which are also present on the limbs and head. The under parts and areas of the face are whitish. The pattern of broken stripes helps to conceal the tiger in its jungle background.

The tiger is mainly nocturnal and preys on animals up to the size of a buffalo. There are 2–3 cubs to a litter as a rule. **35d**

Indian rhinoceros   *Rhinoceros unicornis*   PERISSODACTYLA
Of the 3 Asian species of rhinoceros, the Indian is the largest. It is found in a few areas of riverine grassland in Assam and Nepal but is becoming increasingly rare.

It stands about 183cm high at the shoulder and is 366–427cm long with a tail of another 60cm. It weighs up to 4 tonnes. The hide is blackish grey and deep folds and tubercles give it the appearance of being divided into riveted armoured plates. The legs are short and stout and the feet all have 3 toes. The ears are large with tufted tips and there is a single nasal horn.

A single calf is born. **35e**

Moon rat   *Echinosorex gymnurus*   INSECTIVORA
This animal is not a rat at all but a close relation of the hedgehog. It is found in southern Asia, Sumatra and Borneo.

It is 25–46cm long with a tail of a further 20cm and it weighs 0.9–1.4kg. It is covered in rough black hair with white patches on the head and shoulders and it exudes a smell of rotten onions. The ears are naked and the long snout has many whiskers. The teeth are sharply cusped.

It is nocturnal, feeding mainly on insects but occasionally on frogs and small reptiles. It is solitary in habit, living in hollow logs or crevices. **35f**

SOUTH AMERICA

Common vampire bat   *Desmodus rotundus*   CHIROPTERA
This is the larger of the 2 species of vampire bat in South America. It ranges from Mexico to Paraguay and lives in caves or hollow trees.

The body is up to 7.5cm long, reddish brown above and yellow-brown below. It has no tail. The muzzle is short and conical and the dentition is much reduced. The cheek teeth are small and functionless but the 2 sharp chisel-like upper incisors are used to rasp away the skin of the prey until the blood flows. The bat feeds entirely on fresh blood.

Domesticated animals, and sometimes man, fall victim to this bat. Because of its feeding habits, it can transmit disease, particularly rabies, and is therefore extremely dangerous. **36a**

Weeper capuchin   *Cebus nigrivittatus*   PRIMATES
The capuchins, like all New World monkeys, have tails which are prehensile, at least to some degree, and more teeth than Old World monkeys. The hair framing the face resembles the cowl worn by Capuchin monks – hence the name. The weeper or black-capped capuchin lives mainly in Brazil, Guyana and French Guiana, in large troops in the forests.

It is reddish or greyish brown with darker blackish brown on the outsides of the arms and legs and on the crown of the head. The face and cheeks are pinkish, with white forehead, cheek fringe, throat and chest.

It feeds mainly on fruit. 1–2 young are born after a gestation of $4-4\frac{1}{2}$ months. **36b**

White-nosed coati   *Nasua narica*   CARNIVORA
The coati ranges from the north of South America into the southern USA.

It is similar to a raccoon, with an elongated reddish brown body, about 60cm long, and a long tail ringed with black. The long tapering snout and lower legs are also black. The females and young roam in bands of 5–12. The male, except in the breeding season, is solitary and is known as a 'coatimundi'.

The coati feeds on insects, birds, lizards and fruit and sleeps in trees at night. The young, 4–5 in number, are born in a tree-nest after 77 days' gestation. **36c**

Capybara   *Hydrochaerus hydrochaeris*   RODENTIA
The capybara is the largest living rodent and can be seen in large groups on river banks and lake shores in Central and South America. It is semi-aquatic and looks rather like a cross between a guinea pig and a hippopotamus.

It grows up to 122cm long, weighs up to 45kg and stands 53cm high at the shoulder. The head is broad with short rounded ears. The feet are slightly webbed. The male has a raised gland on the centre of the snout. The hair is short and coarse and fawny brown in colour.

Grass and aquatic vegetation constitute the diet. The capybara is nocturnal, spending the day in muddy hollows. It is an excellent swimmer. **36d**

Giant armadillo   *Priodontes giganteus*   EDENTATA

The giant armadillo, which is closely related to the anteaters and sloths, lives in the dense forests of the Amazon Basin.

Including the tail, it can reach a length of 152cm and weighs up to 45kg. The legs, back and tail are heavily armoured. There are 5 digits on each foot; those of the fore feet have long curved claws, especially the third digit. These are used for slashing open the nests of ants and termites. The insects are then trapped by the long sticky tongue. The armadillo can walk on its hind legs, using its tail to balance.

The principal means of defence is by burrowing. Apart from insects, roots, worms, reptiles and carrion are also eaten. **36e**

Golden agouti   *Dasyprocta aguti*   RODENTIA

This agouti is found in the forests of much of French Guiana and Brazil, where it lives in hollow tree trunks or burrows.

It is about 46cm long with a rudimentary tail. The body is slender and covered in short golden to olive-brown hair. The hair is longer and brighter on the hind quarters and there is a streak of white or yellow in the middle of the under parts. The tail is naked. The toes, of which there are 3 on the hind feet, have flat hoof-like claws. The ears are large and pinkish.

It lives in pairs or small groups, emerging at dusk to forage for fern roots, foliage, fallen fruit and nuts. There are 5–6 young in a litter and usually 2 litters a year. The gestation period is 64 days. **36f**

Red-faced spider monkey   *Ateles paniscus*   PRIMATES

The red-faced or black spider monkey lives in small groups in the Brazilian forests and is almost entirely arboreal.

It has a slender body, about 60cm long, and a long prehensile tail of up to 76cm. The tail has a naked tip and is truly prehensile. The long limbs serve mainly as hooks for swimming and climbing. The fur is coarse and wiry without a soft under fur and generally black in colour. The face and chin are naked and pinkish brown.

Its flesh is considered a great delicacy by local people. **37a**

Kinkajou   *Potus flavus*   CARNIVORA

This member of the raccoon family lives in the forests of Central and South America.

It is about 91cm long overall, with a blunt head, large eyes and rounded ears. The body is slender with short thick legs and a long curling prehensile tail. The short dense fur is a uniform pale yellowish brown with darker markings around the head and ears.

It is arboreal in habit, sleeping in a hollow tree by day and feeding on fruit, honey, shoots and the occasional bird at night. **37b**

Golden lion marmoset   *Leontideus rosalia*   PRIMATES
This marmoset lives in the forests of Brazil and Colombia, north to Panama.

It is about 30cm long with a tail of 45cm. The head is rather leonine and the ears, although large, are hidden in the thick mane. The silky fur is generally rich golden yellow although paler, creamier yellow specimens are found. The head and limbs are usually darker and the face, ears, hands and feet are purple-hued. The hands and feet are exceptionally long and delicate and all digits but the big toes are clawed.

It is gregarious, living in large troops in the tree-tops where it feeds on fruit and insects. It has a shrill twittering cry. **37c**

Jaguar   *Panthera onca*   CARNIVORA
The jaguar is found from New Mexico southwards to Paraguay in forested country.

It is of heavier build than the leopard. A fully grown male is up to 152cm long with a tail of 60cm. It stands 71cm high at the shoulder. It is similar to a leopard in colour but the dark rosette-like spots are larger. The head is also larger. The legs are short and stout and the hind legs are longer than the fore legs.

It preys on turtles, capybaras and sometimes domestic stock. It is arboreal and often catches prey by dropping from a tree. It also catches fish. There are 2–4 young in a litter and the gestation period is 100 days. **37d**

Black-tailed marmoset   *Callithrix melanura*   PRIMATES
The marmosets are among the smallest Primates and are confined to Central and South America. The black-tailed marmoset lives in the forests of Brazil.

It is about the size of a large rat and is distinguished by its large naked ears and its black tail. The fur is long and silky, either grey-brown, with white fronts to the thighs, or a pure white. The face is naked with a fringe of white hairs on the cheeks. The hands and feet are also naked with pointed claws on all digits except the big toe. The feet are much longer than the hands.

It feeds on fruit and insects and has 2–3 young at a birth. **37e**

Red howler monkey   *Alouatta seniculus*   PRIMATES
The red howler monkey lives in troops in the tree tops from Venezuela to Peru and western Brazil. It is especially numerous in the Amazon forest.

It is about the size of a large dog and is reddish chestnut to purplish red in colour. The face, hands, and under side of the tip of the prehensile tail are naked. The back of the skull is flattened, the muzzle protrudes and there is a conspicuous beard. The body hair becomes longer, softer and silkier with age. Its raucous cries are produced from a sound-box of enlarged bones in the swollen throat. They can be heard 3–4km away. **37f**

Tamandua   *Tamandua tetradactyla*   EDENTATA
The tamandua or lesser anteater lives in dense forest and ranges from Mexico to Paraguay and Peru.

It is about 60cm long with a tail of another 40cm. The head is elongated and the mouth has no teeth. The long tongue is kept sticky by the secretion from the salivary gland. The fore feet each have 5 toes with long claws for ripping open the nests of ants and termites. The coat is of a coarse buff-coloured fur with black markings on the throat and shoulders and back.

It is nocturnal, spending the day in thick vegetation or in holes. It can also climb trees. The young are carried on the back of the mother until able to fend for themselves. **38a**

Paca   *Cuniculus paca*   RODENTIA
The paca is found near rivers and streams in forested areas from Mexico to Paraguay.

It is similar to the agouti but the body is heavier and more compact, the hind feet are 5-toed and the skull is strangely shaped. The latter feature, together with the cheek pouches, gives the animal unique sound-producing capabilities. In colour, the paca is light to dark brown with distinctive rows of spots along the sides and pale under parts.

It lives in burrows 1.2–1.5m deep, along river banks, generally in pairs. It feeds at night on fruit and various vegetable matter. 1–2 young are born in a litter. **38b**

Woolly opossum   *Caluromys lanatus*   MARSUPIALIA
This opossum is found throughout tropical South America, where it fills an ecological niche similar to that of the phalangers of Australia.

It is the size of a large rat with a fully prehensile tail, naked for much of its length and about 50cm long. The fur is dense and golden brown in colour with paler under parts. The ears are large and the eyes, which are big and protuberant, are most efficient at dawn and dusk.

The opossum feeds on insects, small vertebrates, carrion, leaves and fruit. Although it is a marsupial, it lacks a pouch and the young cling first to the nipples and then to the back of the female. **38c**

Ocelot *Felis pardalis* CARNIVORA
The ocelot is found from Texas and Mexico in the north, southwards to Ecuador, Brazil and Paraguay.

A fully grown male is up to 122cm long, including the tail of 38cm. It weighs up to 16kg. The fur varies from tawny yellow to brownish grey, with a conspicuous pattern of dark spots and blotches. The ears are black and the tail is ringed.

It is an excellent climber and spends a great deal of time in the trees where it preys on birds, mammals, frogs and reptiles. It is nocturnal and lives alone or in pairs. The gestation period is 90 days and 2 cubs are generally born at a time. **38d**

White-lipped peccary *Tayassu albirostris* ARTIODACTYLA
The white-lipped peccary lives in herds, deep in the forest, and ranges from Mexico to Paraguay.

It is related to the pig, which it closely resembles. About 91cm long, it stands 60cm high at the shoulder. The body is covered with bristle-like hairs which form a slight mane on the neck. It has white lips and a white moustache. There is a scent gland in the middle of the back which is exposed when the hair on the back is raised. There are 2 pairs of tusks, one in each jaw. The upper pair are short and downward curving with cutting edges.

It feeds on fruit, roots, carrion, worms and insects. **38e**

Two-toed sloth *Choloepus didactylus* EDENTATA
The two-toed sloth or unau lives in the forests of the Amazon Basin in Brazil.

It has 2 toes on each fore foot (the three-toed sloth, *Bradypus tridactylus*, has 3). Just over 60cm long, this sloth has a short rounded head, small scarcely visible ears and a rudimentary tail. The thick long fur is brownish grey. The fore limbs are much longer than the hind limbs but in each case the feet are long and slender with long curved claws.

Chiefly an arboreal creature, this sloth hangs upside down from branches when on the move and curls up in them when asleep. It moves sluggishly and continuously. It can also drag itself along the ground by its fore feet. It feeds on leaves and foliage, particularly of the cecropia tree. **38f**

AFRICA

Potto   *Perodicticus potto*   PRIMATES

The potto lives in the lower levels of the forests of west, central and east Africa.

It is about the size of a squirrel and weighs about 1.4kg. It has a round head with a blunt naked muzzle, short round ears and large round eyes. The tail is only 2.5cm or so long. The hands and feet are specialised for grasping; the second digit is reduced to a stump and the first digit is opposable and very strong. The dense fur is rufous brown in colour. A row of horny tubercles in the neck region cover the spines of the vertebrae.

A nocturnal creature, the potto feeds on insects, fruit, berries and small birds. The single young clings to the mother's stomach. **39a**

Red colobus monkey   *Colobus badius*   PRIMATES

The red colobus is one of the leaf-eating monkeys and is widespread in the forests of west Africa and the Congo Basin. The colobus monkeys have a distinctive vestigial thumb.

It lives in the upper storeys of the forest and has long limbs for leaping from tree to tree and a prehensile tail. The body is covered with long silky black fur and the head, arms and legs are various shades of red from chestnut and orange through to mahogany and brown.

The colobus moves in troops through the trees, gathering leaves, lichens and fruit. **39b**

African brush-tailed porcupine   *Atherurus africanus*   RODENTIA

This species of porcupine lives, generally near water, in the tropical forests of central Africa.

It is about 53cm long, greyish in colour and covered with flattened spines. The distinctive long scaly tail is about 23cm long and ends in a thick tuft of bristles.

It seldom climbs trees and spends the day in its burrow. At night, it forages in groups for tubers, fruit and vegetation. **39c**

Small-scaled tree pangolin   *Manis tricuspis*   PHOLIDOTA
The tree pangolin lives in the forests of west Africa and ranges eastwards into Uganda.

It resembles a pine cone, tapered at both ends, with flat overlapping scales, horny in texture and made of fused hair. The head and body are about 25cm long and the tail is a further 63cm. For defence, it rolls into a ball, raising the sharp edges of the scales. The tail is an effective weapon and the pangolin can also discharge a noxious fluid. The claws of the fore feet are used to open termite nests. The insects are then collected on the long sticky tongue.

1–2 offspring are born each year and they travel on the mother's tail until able to fend for themselves. **39d**

Chequered elephant shrew   *Rhynchocyon cirnei*   INSECTIVORA
This species of elephant shrew is found in central Africa from Zaire to Kenya and Tanzania.

It is about 28cm long with a tail of a further 23cm. The fur is hazel to reddish brown in colour on the back, with rows of evenly spaced squarish spots. The ears and eyes are large and the nose is elongated and flexible. There is a scent gland on the under side of the tail.

The shrew is active during the day and feeds on insects which it extracts from crevices with its nose. 1–2 young are born in the spring. **39e**

Okapi   *Okapia johnstoni*   ARTIODACTYLA
The okapi lives in dense forests in the Congo Basin. A relative of the giraffe, it was discovered by Sir Harry Johnston, in 1900.

It stands about 152cm high at the shoulders. The hide is dark reddish brown, striped with white on the upper hind legs and upper fore legs. The lower legs are white with black markings. The tail is relatively short and ends in a dark bushy tuft. The head is long and the ears broad. The male has 2 short skin-covered horns with naked tips.

Because of its short neck, the okapi feeds on leaves from the lower parts of trees; these it gathers with its long tongue. **39f**

Bushpig   *Potamochoerus porcus*   ARTIODACTYLA
The bushpig or Red River hog is found throughout most of Africa south of the Sahara. It lives in dense bush and reed beds.

It stands up to 76cm at the shoulder and has an elongated head with a warty face and long pointed ears. The coat is brownish red with flat bristles and an erect crest down the back. The tail is relatively short and tufted at the tip.

It is nocturnal, moving in herds of up to 24, and feeding on roots, grasses and fruits. The young, 6–8 per litter, are marked with longitudinal brown and yellow stripes. **40a**

African civet   *Viverra civetta*   CARNIVORA
This civet is found in overgrown country near rivers and swamps south of the Sahara.

It is heavily built, with a long body (85cm) and a tail of 46cm. The long limbs, cheeks and throat, and also the erectile crest of hair along the back, are black. There are glands at the base of the tail.

It is nocturnal in habit, spending the day in old aardvark burrows. Hares, reptiles, insects, carrion and some vegetable matter form the principle diet. It lives alone or in pairs. There are 2–3 young in a litter. **40b**

Senegal bushbaby   *Galago senegalensis*   PRIMATES
This bushbaby is widespread in the tropical rain forest of Africa.

It is about the size of a squirrel with a broad head, very large eyes, and pointed muzzle. The ears are very large and naked. The coat is pale grey with white under parts and a grey to yellowish brown tail. The tarsal bones are greatly elongated, enabling it to leap up to 10m, and the digits have pads for gripping. An extremely agile tree-dweller, the bushbaby is nocturnal, feeding on fruit and insects. **40c**

Chimpanzee   *Pan troglodytes*   PRIMATES
There are several local races of chimpanzee inhabiting the tropical forests from Sierra Leone in the west to Uganda in the east.

A fully grown male is 122–153cm high; the females are smaller. The long hair is generally black with short white hairs on the lower face and chin. The face is naked, flesh-coloured at birth but becoming brownish yellow with age. The hands and feet are also naked and there is no obvious tail. It feeds on fruit and tree shoots, but may take eggs and small birds.

The female produces a single young at a birth. The chimpanzee may live for up to 35 years and is the most intelligent of the apes. **40d**

Water chevrotain   *Hyemoschus aquaticus*   ARTIODACTYLA
This African species of chevrotain or mouse deer is found near water in the forests of Zaire and Cameroon.

It is more heavily built than the Asian chevrotains, stands about 36cm at the shoulder and is up to 90cm long. The coat is brown with white markings on the chest and throat. The legs are long and slender and the head is small with a pointed snout. Neither sex has horns but the male has long, tusk-like canines.

The chevrotain spends the day in holes or crevices and emerges at night to feed on vegetation and fruit. **40e**

Bushbuck   *Tragelaphus scriptus*   ARTIODACTYLA
The bushbuck, or harnessed antelope, is found in most parts of Africa south of the Sahara.

The male is 76–91cm high at the shoulder and weighs about 68kg. The male has spirally twisted horns, 30–43cm long. Body colour varies according to race but is generally dark reddish brown with white spots on the flanks and a black and white crest along the midline of the back. The female is smaller and fox-red with more abundant white markings.

It is solitary and mainly nocturnal, browsing on leaves, tender shoots and pods. The gestation period is 180–255 days. **40f**

Mandrill   *Mandrillus sphinx*   PRIMATES
The mandrill lives in the forests of west Africa and is particularly abundant around the Gulf of Guinea.

The male has a very distinctive face with sausage-like swellings on either side of the muzzle, bearing transverse purple-bluish grooves and separated by a central ridge of bright vermilion which extends to the tip of the nose. The fur is blackish olive on the body, with darker patches on the head, spine and nape of the neck. The buttocks have a violet patch and the hind parts are bare and reddish in colour. The eyes are hazel and the beard is yellow. The crest of hair on the crown makes the face appear longer. The tail is a mere stump, naked underneath. **41a**

Gorilla   *Gorilla gorilla*   PRIMATES
There are 2 races of gorilla: the lowland form of west Africa and Cameroon and the mountain form of the eastern Congo Basin.

A fully grown male is up to 183cm high and weighs up to 205kg. The female is smaller. It has distinctive brow ridges over the eyes, small ears and long arms. The wide strong hands have callosities on the backs, where the hand is doubled over and meets the ground during walking. The neck is short and thick and the crown of the head rises to a conspicuous crest. The long hair and the bare skin of the face, hands and feet are black. The body hair becomes grizzled with age.

The gorilla roams the forest during the day in small family groups, searching for fruit and plants, and spends the nights in trees. **41b**

Black mangabey   *Cercocebus aterrimus*   PRIMATES
The mangabeys are the African equivalents of the Asiatic macaques. The black mangabey is found in the rain forest south of the Congo.

It is larger than the average monkey, with a long, non-prehensile tail and long limbs, by means of which it swings through the trees. The buttocks are covered with calloused skin, on which the mangabey sits.

It is almost entirely arboreal and lives in the upper stories of the forest, where it travels about in large troops, feeding on fruit. **41c**

Red duiker   *Cephalophus natalensis*   ARTIODACTYLA
Duikers are a group of small antelopes, common over much of Africa south of the Sahara, in forest and bush country.

The red or Natal duiker is about 60cm high at the shoulder and is a uniform chestnut red. The erect horns are 7.5–10cm long and found in both sexes. There is a tuft of long hair between the horns. The ears are shorter and broader than in other duikers. The tail is short and untufted. **41d**

Giant forest hog   *Hylochoerus meinertzhageni*   ARTIODACTYLA
This animal, the largest living pig, lives so deep in the forests of Kenya and the Congo Basin that it remained undiscovered by Europeans until 1894.

An adult male is up to 152cm long and 91cm high at the shoulder. It can weigh up to 136kg. It is a uniform brownish black with sparse hair, except for the tufts at the base of each widespread ear and at the tip of the tail, and for the crest on the back of the head. There is a round depression on the forehead and a pair of long naked projections in front of the eyes. The muzzle terminates in a large terminal disc. The upper and lower tusks are up to 23cm long.

The forest hog lives in small family parties and is active mainly at dawn and dusk. It browses on low bushes but also takes small mammals and birds. **41e**

MALAGASY REPUBLIC (MADAGASCAR)

Galidia   *Galidia elegans*   CARNIVORA
The galidia, vontsira or ring-tailed mongoose is found only in the Malagasy Republic.

It is a graceful squirrel-like animal, closely related to the civets and is about 38cm long. The coat is a bright reddish brown.

Unlike the civets, it is active during the day, moving alone or in pairs through the trees and feeding on locusts, beetles, lizards, reptiles and amphibians. **42a**

Aye aye   *Daubentonia madagascariensis*   PRIMATES
The aye aye is found in the northern forests but is now becoming exceedingly rare.

It was formerly considered to be a type of squirrel because of its teeth but, because of its opposable thumbs and the nails on the big toes, it is now classed as a primate. About the size of a cat, the aye aye has shaggy black hair and a thick bushy tail. It is arboreal and nocturnal. The eyes are large and the bat-like ears enable it to hear the wood-boring beetle larvae on which it feeds. These larvae are dug out with the specially modified middle finger or with the incisors. It also eats bamboo pith and sugar cane.

The aye aye lives singly or in pairs in a nest or hollow tree. The female makes a special nest in which the single young is born in February–March. **42b**

Ring-tailed lemur   *Lemur catta*   PRIMATES
The lemur family is found only in the Malagasy Republic. The ring-tailed lemur is about 122cm long, including the tail. It is ash grey in colour with paler under parts, face and ears. The muzzle is black and there is a black ring around each eye. The tail is marked with alternate black and white rings.

It spends more time on the ground than in the trees and moves about in small, noisy parties. It hunts in the early evening and at first light for small birds, eggs, small mammals, lizards, snakes and fruit. The female bears 1–3 young per litter. **42c**

Tenrec   *Tenrec ecaudatus*   INSECTIVORA
The tenrec is one of the largest insectivores and is found only in the Malagasy Republic.

It is 30–40cm long. The coat is generally brown in colour, tinged with yellow, and is made up of bristles and coarse hairs with a scattering of flexible spines. The snout is long and flexible.

It roots up worms, grubs and insects from the ground. 12–16 young are produced at a birth. It is nocturnal in habit, burrows underground and remains torpid in hot weather. **42d**

AUSTRALIA/NEW GUINEA

Black tree kangaroo   *Dendrolagus ursinus*   MARSUPIALIA
This close relative of the common kangaroos has limbs modified for an arboreal way of life and is found in the forests of New Guinea.

It is about 60cm long with a tail of 56–60cm. Unlike other kangaroos, its hind legs are only slightly larger than the fore legs. All the toes have strong curved claws which assist in climbing. The thick fur is black although the face is paler. The muzzle is broad and partially bare. The tail is covered with thick fur and is not prehensile. It feeds mainly on leaves and fruit. **43a**

New Guinea spotted cuscus   *Phalanger maculatus*   MARSUPIALIA
This cuscus is found in the very north of Queensland and in New Guinea.

It is about the size of a large cat with a long tail which is covered in fur, apart from the last 15cm, which are naked on the under side and prehensile. The thick woolly fur is grey above and yellowish white below. The male has irregular white markings on the head and body. The blunt head has a fairly pointed snout and the ears are short and covered with hair. The fore and hind limbs are almost equal in length. There are long curved claws on the fore feet and, of the 5 toes on the hind feet, the first is opposable and clawless.

It is a solitary arboreal animal, feeding on fruits, leaves, birds and small mammals. The female produces 2 young at a birth and these remain in the pouch for some time. **43b**

Spotted native cat   *Dasyurops maculatus*   CARNIVORA
This native cat is typical of flesh-eating marsupials and is to be found in both Australia and Tasmania.

It is small, rather rat-like and about 46cm long, including the furry tail. The fur is dark brown generally, with white spots, and golden brown on the muzzle, under parts and legs. The eyes are large as befits a nocturnal animal.

The cat sleeps in crevices during the day, emerging at night to feed on eggs, rats, mice, rabbits and small wallabies. **43c**

New Guinea anteater   *Zaglossus bruijni*   MONOTREMATA
This spiny anteater, which is found only in New Guinea, is closely related to the Australian echidna.

It is larger, reaching a length of up to 76cm and a weight of 16kg. The snout is longer, tapering and curved downwards. The spines are shorter and almost hidden by the dense fur, which varies in colour from light to dark brown. The fore feet have short strong claws for digging and the long (30cm) sticky tongue is used to gather the ants and termites on which it feeds.

It is egg-laying. The 1–3 young are carried in a rudimentary pouch until sufficiently mature. **43d**

Australian flying fox   *Pteropus poliocephalus*   INSECTIVORA
This fruit bat is the largest of the Australian bats and is found in the rain forest of northern Queensland. It is one of the many species of fruit bats which occur throughout India, Peninsular Malaysia and Indonesia.

The body is about 30cm long and is covered in thick pale brown fur with a russet 'collar' around the neck and shoulders. The eyes are large and the wings have a span of up to 120 cm. There is a claw on the tip of the second finger.

This bat forms great flocks which roost during the day and feed on fruit at night, often causing great damage to crops. **43e**

7
Mountains

Mountains occur throughout the world in most climatic and vegetation zones. They are the result of movements of the earth's crust and are classified according to the way in which they were formed.

The greatest ranges are the *fold* mountains, e.g. the Great Dividing Range of Australia, Rocky Mountains of North America, Andes of South America (which lie in a north-south direction), Pyrenees and Himalayas (which lie in an east-west direction). Their orientation is significant in terms of animal distribution. The former tend to allow species from colder latitudes to extend their range towards the Equator (the bighorn sheep ranges from Alaska to Mexico) whereas the latter act as a barrier. There are also the *block* mountain ranges, such as the Vosges and the Black Forest of Europe, and the peak-like *residual* mountains, such as Mt Kinabalu, Borneo, and Mt Kenya, Africa, which stand up like islands above the 'sea' of the surrounding countryside. Where the tops of the mountains have been worn away, high plateaux, such as those of the Andes and Tibet, are left.

Although widely scattered geographically, mountains have certain features in common. For every 1km of altitude the temperature falls by 0.5–1°C. This means that, at the Equator, there are night frosts at 3350m. The warm season also gets shorter with increasing altitude. Rainfall depends on aspect and wind direction. The coastal ranges which receive moisture-laden winds have a high rate of precipitation on the seaward side, as the winds are forced to rise and lose their moisture as they cool. By the time the winds have passed over the mountains they are carrying very little moisture and the landward side of the mountains get a much reduced rainfall. Pressure also decreases with altitude and so the atmosphere becomes rarer.

Increasing altitude has the same effect as increasing latitude on vegetation and causes a similar zonation: grassland, deciduous forest, coniferous forest. At the upper limit of the forest, or *tree-line*, there is a peculiarly mountain vegetation known as the *alpine zone*. This may consist of scattered mountain pine, dwarf shrubs and alpine meadows, or of a tundra-like vegetation, and it extends as far as the *snow-line*, above which there is permanent snow. On mountains where temperature extremes, exposure, too little or too much rain, and extremely resistant rock inhibit soil formation and therefore plant growth, the terrain is steep, barren and rocky.

The animals of these zones in the mountains show adaptations similar to their counterparts in equivalent zones in other latitudes. Conditions in the alpine zone are harsh and there are relatively few species. Adaptations are to withstand the cold. Bodies are stout and stocky, extremities and limbs are smaller, fur is thick and insulating. The marmots and chipmunk of the alpine meadows live in deep burrows where the marmots hibernate in the winter. In the cold windswept high plateaux, the Tibetan yak has an extremely thick shaggy coat as do the llamas, vicunas and guanacoes of South America. The latter group, like the closely related camel, can withstand dehydration. They are also known to have an increased number of red cells in their blood which enables them to increase their oxygen uptake in the rarified atmosphere.

On the steep barren mountainsides there are goats, sheep and deer, e.g. chamois, ibex, argali These animals, with their stocky muscular legs and small hooves, are adapted for leaping from crag to crag and balancing precariously. Carnivores are relatively few.

NORTH AMERICA

Puma   *Felis concolor*   CARNIVORA

The puma or cougar ranges from the mountainous parts of western Canada southwards to Patagonia. It prefers well wooded hilly districts but is also found on the pampas.

A fully grown male is about 150cm long, with a tail of 60–76cm, and weighs up to 118kg. It is yellowish brown above with paler under parts but local races vary, being more reddish or greyish. The ears are dark on the outside with a whitish inside and there are patches of white on the lips, divided on the upper lip by a conspicuous dark streak. The tail is thick and rounded with a dark tip.

It lives mainly with its mate. There are usually 2 cubs in a litter but sometimes as many as 5. They have dark spots for about 6 months. The gestation period is 90–93 days. **44a**

Alpine chipmunk   *Tamias alpinus*   RODENTIA

This species of chipmunk is found in the alpine meadows 2700–4000m up in the Sierra Nevada of California.

It is squirrel-like, about 18cm long, with a black-tipped bushy tail.

It is pale in colour with dark brown and white stripes running along the back and also across the eye.

It constructs a long (up to 1m) tunnel which leads to a grass-lined nest chamber. Here it stores nuts, seeds, fruit and berries, which it transports in its cheek pouches, for the winter. About 6 young are born after 35 days' gestation. **44b**

Rocky Mountain goat   *Oreamnos americanus*   ARTIODACTYLA
This goat lives in small herds on the steep mountain sides and cliffs of British Columbia, Alberta, Idaho and Montana.

It has a short neck and a large head. The fur is long and thick and pure white and, with the dense layer of body fat, protects against the cold. The shoulders are higher (89–101cm in the male) than the rump. The male weighs from 90–135kg. The female is slightly smaller but both have horns and beards. The horns are black and upright, curving back slightly at the tips and up to 23cm long. The short stocky legs have small hoofs.

It feeds on grass, lichens and twigs and 1–2 kids are born in April or May. **44c**

Dall's sheep   *Ovis dalli*   ARTIODACTYLA
Dall's sheep, also known as the white sheep, is a northern race of the bighorn and is found in Alaska and western Canada.

It is smaller than the bighorn and the horns are much more widely spread. The coat is thick and heavy, usually entirely white but sometimes darker above. Glands on the feet leave a scent trail for other sheep to follow. In its feeding and reproduction, it resembles the bighorn. **44d**

Hoary marmot   *Marmota caligata*   RODENTIA
This large rodent is found in the mountains of Alaska and western North America in the grassy areas between the tree-line and the snow-line.

It is about 60cm long with a tail of a further 15cm and can weigh up to 8kg. The body is stockily built with short limbs and a broad head. The hoary marmot is so-called because its long dense fur is greyish white in colour. The lower legs and feet are black.

It is colonial in habit and lives in grass-lined nest chambers at the end of long (3m) burrows. It feeds on vegetation and roots in the summer, storing up reserves of body fat for hibernation. Breeding does not occur until the third year of life. 1 litter of 2–4 young is born every 2 years. **44e**

Bighorn   *Ovis canadensis*   ARTIODACTYLA
The bighorn or Rocky Mountain sheep, the only wild sheep in America, occurs as several local races at high altitudes in the Rocky Mountains from Alaska to Mexico.

A fully grown ram stands up to 106cm at the shoulder with massive horns which grow upwards from the skull and curve backwards and downwards to a curled point. The horns may measure up to 114cm around the curve. The ewe is smaller with short, pointed, almost straight horns. The fleece varies from almost pure white to blackish grey according to locality. The under parts are white and there is a conspicuous white rump patch. The short tail is black above and white below.

It moves about in flocks, feeding on grass and available vegetation. The ewe produces 1–2 lambs after a gestation of 180 days. **44f**

EURASIA

Alpine marmot   *Marmota marmota*   RODENTIA
The alpine marmot is found only in the Alps, Pyrenees and Carpathians, where it lives in colonies not far from the snow-line. During winter the colonies hibernate in large burrows.

It is closely related to the squirrels and is about 46–51cm long with a tail of a further 13–15cm. The head is short and wide with small, rounded ears and large eyes. The short legs end in 5-toed feet, although the first toe of the fore foot is much shorter than the others. The fur is rather coarse, dark brown above with a reddish brown neck and under parts and greyish flanks.

It feeds mainly on leaves and grass, and roots when available. Normally 2–5 young are born at a time. **45a**

Wild yak   *Bos mutus*   ARTIODACTYLA
This species of wild cattle inhabits the upland areas of central Asia, at altitudes of 5500–6100m in parts of Tibet.

It stands about 168cm high at the shoulder and has a long, shaggy, brownish black coat which reaches almost to the hooves. The tail is very bushy and the muzzle is greyish. The long horns curve upwards and outwards from the head.

Domesticated breeds are smaller, with shorter horns, and are very variable in colour. They are used for transport and haulage and are also valued for their milk. **45b**

Chamois   *Rupicapra rupicapra*   ARTIODACTYLA

The chamois lives near the tree-line in the Alps, Appennines, Carpathians and parts of Asia Minor, where it feeds on the sparse mountain vegetation.

The body is about 122cm long and 81cm high at the shoulders. The legs are fairly long and stoutly built and the hoofs are adapted to negotiate slippery surfaces. The short (20–25cm) horns are found in both sexes. They rise almost at right angles to the forehead then bend backwards and downwards in a sharp hook. In summer the fur is reddish brown with yellowish under parts and a black stripe along the back. It darkens to almost black above in winter, with white under parts.

1–3 kids are born in May–June. **45c**

Snow leopard   *Panthera uncia*   CARNIVORA

The snow leopard or ounce is found in rocky grassland between the tree and snow-lines in the Altai Mountains and the Himalayas.

It is a medium-sized cat about 106cm long, with a tail of a further 91cm. An adult male weighs about 91kg. The fur is a pale ashy brown, marked with black rosettes, and is very long – 5cm on the back and up to 10cm on the under parts – as protection from the cold.

It feeds on small rodents and also goats, sheep, musk deer and wild boar. It makes a den in the rocks and here the 2–3 young are born in April. **45d**

Argali   *Ovis ammon*   ARTIODACTYLA

The argali is found in central Asia, from Altai and Bokhara to Tibet and Mongolia, where it inhabits rocky mountainous country at altitudes of 900–1200m.

It is the largest sheep, standing up to 122cm at the shoulders. The huge horns, whose front faces are heavily wrinkled, grow outwards and downwards in an open spiral. The coat is greyish brown above and white beneath but becomes longer, thicker and darker in the winter. The male usually has a whitish patch on the rump, a whitish face and whitish inner sides to the legs.

The ewes and lambs live in large flocks. The immature rams live apart in small groups. **45e**

Alpine ibex   *Capra ibex ibex*   ARTIODACTYLA

This ibex, a close relation of the Nubian ibex of Africa, was once nearly extinct, apart from a colony in northern Italy, but it is now becoming re-established.

A species of goat, it stands 101cm high at the shoulder and is brownish grey in colour. The male has a neat short beard and curved horns up to 76cm long. The horns in the female are much smaller – up to 20cm long.

It lives on cliffs and crags close to the snow line and feeds on grass and lichens. The young are born in the spring after 158 days' gestation. **45f**

SOUTH AMERICA

Chinchilla   *Chinchilla laniger*   RODENTIA
The chinchilla lives in barren rocky places, semi-deserts and on the mountain sides in the Peruvian Andes.

It is squirrel-like, about 25cm long with a tail of about the same length. It has long hind limbs and a long bushy tail. The head is pointed and the ears are large, delicate and cup-like. The soft silky fur is about 2.5cm long, pearly grey on the back and sides and whitish on the under parts. Because its fur is so highly prized, the chinchilla is now strictly protected.

It feeds mainly on roots, grasses and moss. There are up to 3 litters a year, each of 1–4 young. **46a**

Spectacled bear   *Tremarctos ornatus*   CARNIVORA
The spectacled bear is found in the Andes from southern Venezuela to Chile but is now becoming very rare.

The body is about 122cm long and is almost black in colour. Its name derives from the narrow white stripe which passes from behind the eye, along the side of the muzzle, forward to the bridge of the nose then down across the cheek to the throat and chest.

It subsists mainly on vegetation, particularly fruit, nuts and buds. **46b**

Vicuna   *Vicugna vicugna*   ARTIODACTYLA
The vicuna is the smallest of the South American camels. It lives on the high plateaux of the Andes, near to the snow-line, in Argentina, Bolivia, Chile and Peru.

It is about 76cm high and weighs 45kg or so. It is golden fawn in colour with a white patch on the lower throat. Despite the fine quality of the wool, the vicuna has never been domesticated successfully.

The females form herds of 8–12 under the leadership of one male and the other males herd together. Grasses and broad-leaved herbs form the diet and water is taken every 2 days. A single offspring is born after 10 months. **46c**

Llama   *Lama glama*   ARTIODACTYLA
The llama, which is found in the high Andes from Ecuador to Patagonia, is a domesticated form of the wild guanaco. It has been used since Inca times as a beast of burden and a source of milk.

It stands about 122cm high at the shoulder and is about 183cm long. The coat is thick and woolly and shows great variation in colour: reddish brown, white, yellowish white, blackish and sometimes piebald.

Mating occurs in August–September and the single young is born after 10–11 months' gestation. **46d**

Guanaco   *Lama guanicoe*   ARTIODACTYLA
The guanaco is found from sea-level up to 4000m along the west coast of South America, most commonly in semi-desert and on high altitude plains. It is a swift runner but not as good a climber as the vicuna.

It is the tallest mammal in South America, standing some 109cm high, and it weighs up to 90kg. The coat is thick to keep the animal warm and is pale brown in colour, darker on the face and paler beneath. Because of the rarity of the atmosphere, there are a great number of red cells in the blood to increase oxygen uptake.

The female moves in herds of 4–10, led by a male. The other males form herds of 12–50. **46e**

AFRICA

Barbary sheep   *Ammotragus lervia*   ARTIODACTYLA
The Barbary sheep or aoudad is the only wild sheep in Africa and it lives in bare sandy and rocky areas of the mountains in the north.

It is 101cm high at the shoulder and has smooth curved semi-circular horns up to 76cm long. The horns in the female are only slightly smaller. The head is long and the ears relatively large. The male has a fringe of long hair hanging from the throat and chest. The colour is a uniform tawny grey.

It moves in small groups feeding on vegetation, grass and lichens and drinks only every 4–5 days. 1–2 young are born after 160 days' gestation. **47a**

Nubian ibex   *Capra ibex nubiana*   ARTIODACTYLA
This goat is found in rocky, hilly country in Egypt, Sinai and parts of Arabia.

It is up to 91cm high at the shoulder and about 125cm long, with a short tail of 15cm. The female is generally smaller. The horns are long (up to 122cm) and curved, rising almost in the plane of the forehead and sweeping upwards and backwards. The front surface has a series of transverse ridges which are indicators of age. **47b**

Cape mountain zebra   *Equus zebra*   PERISSODACTYLA
This gregarious animal was once common over much of southern Africa, especially in Cape Province. Most are now found only in reserves.

It is one of several types of zebra and has the familiar striped coat. The stripes are vertical on the body as far as the crupper where they merge with the horizontal stripes on the hindquarters. There is a narrow stripe in the middle of the back. It is black and fawny white with a black mane on the neck. The ears are long and the muzzle is dark. **47c**

8
Oceans

The ocean, of which the Atlantic, Indian and Pacific Oceans make up by far the largest part, covers almost 71% of the Earth's surface to a mean depth of about 3km. One of the most remarkable features of this immense body of salt water is its constancy. There are no seasonal effects as such, except possibly on its margins, and it is inhabited throughout most of its volume.

The deepest part, the *abyssal zone*, is always dark; the temperature, although low, is constant and the pressure of the water is considerable. The surface layers and the shallow coastal waters experience a greater variety of conditions. The heat of the sun warms up the water, wind action produces waves, and rainfall, particularly in equatorial regions, may be sufficient to reduce salinity. In polar regions, ice formation has the effect of increasing salinity and, because the ice floats on the surface, it also acts as an insulating layer. Apart from the action of the wind stirring up the surface layers, the forces exerted by the sun and moon and the rotation of the earth generate tides and currents and the effects of these extend into the deeper waters.

Because of the dissolved salts and sunlight, the ocean supports abundant plant life, mainly in the form of microscopic cells, which float in the surface waters. These are called *phytoplankton*. In shallow coastal waters, wherever the light can penetrate, the sea-weeds grow.

The mammals which live in the sea have evolved from land creatures and have adapted to their new environment with varying degrees of success. The seals and sea-lions must return to land to breed and bear their young and they do not venture far out to sea. The dugong, although it spends its entire life in the sea, remains in coastal waters. The whales and dolphins, however, inhabit the open water and are completely independent of the land.

In order to move through the water more efficiently, the bodies of all these mammals have become stream-lined and the limbs have developed into flippers or fins for propulsion. The hind flippers in sea-lions can be turned under the body to help movement on land; the seals, which are more fully aquatic, have lost this ability and, in the dugong, whales and dolphins, there is a crescent-shaped tail fin. A layer of body fat, known as *blubber*, facilitates stream-lining and provides insulation.

All mammals are air-breathers and therefore marine mammals must surface to breathe. However, there are various physiological adaptations, mainly of the blood system, which allow them to hold their breath for long periods under water and also to avoid many of the adverse effects of pressure. They can therefore stay under water for considerable periods of time and even dive to very great depths in search of food. It is because they are air-breathers, and because whales and dolphins give birth in open water, that their young, unlike the young of other mammals, are born tail first.

Because the ocean is so vast, and because there are no seasonal shortages of food, there is a wide variety of food sources constantly available. In coastal waters, the seaweed beds, molluscs and fish, and crustaceans respectively support the dugong, the seals and the sea-lions. In open waters, different levels of the ocean are exploited. The right whale filters the planktonic krill from the surface waters, the dolphin catches fish in mid-water and the sperm whale feeds in very deep waters on squid and cuttlefish.

Because of the difficulty in communication over vast distances in the open sea, a system of vocalisations and echo-location has evolved in the whales and dolphins; this system is similar in principle to that of the bats on land.

Common dolphin   *Delphinus delphis*   CETACEA
This dolphin occurs in large schools throughout most of the temperate and warm seas of the world.

A fully grown specimen is 1.8–2.4m long, slender and torpedo-like in shape, with horizontal tail flukes and a recurved dorsal fin. The long narrow beak, armed with teeth, is its distinctive feature. The colour is normally black or brown on the back, and white below with wavy bands of grey, white and yellow on the flanks.

It has a remarkable turn of speed (up to 30 knots) and feeds mainly on fish. The gestation period is 276 days and the female gives birth to a single calf in the summer. **48a**

Sperm whale   *Physeter catodon*   CETACEA
The sperm whale, much reduced in numbers by overhunting, occurs in all tropical waters.

This species belongs to the toothed whales, or Odontoceti. A fully grown male can reach over 18m in length; the females are about half this size. There is no dorsal fin and the flippers are placed just behind the small eyes, which are just behind and above the corner of the mouth. The head is squarish with a blunt, high, truncated muzzle and the lower jaw is very small in proportion. The teeth are up to 20cm long. As in all whales, the tail flukes are horizontal.

The sperm whale feeds mainly on cuttlefish and squid. The gestation period is $14\frac{3}{4}$ months and the single calf is 4.25m long at birth. **48b**

Greenland right whale   *Balaena mysticetus*   CETACEA
Despite its rarity, this species ranges through most of the Arctic Ocean, moving southward in the winter and returning to the north in the summer.

It is about 15.25m long and has no dorsal fin. The flippers are comparatively short and the horizontal tail flukes span about 66cm. The head is enormous, often as much as one third of the length of the body. The jaws are arched above and widely curved below and are provided with the baleen fringes typical of the whalebone whales, or Mysticeti. This whale is generally black in colour, often with white patches on the throat and under parts.

It feeds on krill, a shrimp-like creature, which it filters from the sea water by means of the baleen. Mating takes place in July. After 276 days' gestation, a single 4.6m long calf is born. **48c**

Dugong   *Dugong dugon*   SIRENIA
The dugong is found in the shallow tropical waters of the Red Sea, Indian and Pacific Oceans and the East China Sea.

The adult is 2.1–2.75m long. The animal spends its whole life in water and consequently it has a broad whale-like crescent-shaped tail and well developed fore flippers which, incidentally, lack nails. The male has tusks in the upper jaw. The bones are hard and firm and the skeleton shows similarities to that of the elephant.

The thick fleshy lips and truncated snout are well-suited for browsing on submarine pastures of seaweed. A single calf is produced after a gestation period of 12 months. **48d**

Californian sea-lion   *Zalophus californianus*   PINNIPEDIA
This species occurs over most of the Pacific coastline of North America from California to Mexico.

Sea-lions are distinguished from seals by their small external ears and by their hind flippers, which can be bent forward for support on land. The Californian sea-lion has a narrow convex head, the face dropping sharply below the eyes and curving out to the snout. A fully grown male is 2.1–2.4m long and a large bull weighs up to 227kg. The female is smaller. The colour varies from dark to light brown and the under parts are always darker.

The natural diet is crustaceans but fish are readily accepted by animals in captivity. This species breeds in large colonies on rocky islands, each bull having its own harem of cows. One offspring is born after a gestation period of 342 days. **48e**

Grey seal *Halichoerus grypus* PINNIPEDIA
The grey seal ranges throughout both sides of the North Atlantic Ocean and extends into the Baltic.

Also known as the Atlantic seal, it typifies the true seals by its lack of external ears and its backwardly directed hind feet, which serve as a rudder. A fully grown male measures up to 3.6m in length and weighs about 340kg. The neck is short, as are the front flippers, and all 4 feet have clawed toes. In colour, the seal is silvery to yellowish grey, darker above than below, and often marked with darker spots.

Food consists of fish and molluscs. In the British Isles, mating occurs in November–December and, after 11 months, a single pup weighing about 15kg is produced. **48f**

Bibliography

Buckles, M.P. (1979), *Animals and their world*. Blandford Press, Poole, Dorset.

Duplaix, N. & Simon, N. (1976), *World guide to mammals*. Crown.

Gotch, A.F. (1979), *Mammals — their Latin names explained*. Blandford Press, Poole, Dorset.

MacKinnon, J. & McKinnon, K. (1974), *Animals of Asia. The ecology of the Oriental region*. Eurobook Ltd, London.

Morris, D. (1965), *The mammals. A guide to living species*. Hodder & Stoughton Ltd, Sevenoaks, Kent.

Preece, D.M. & Wood, H.R.B. (1967), *Modern geography series. Book I, Foundations of geography*. University Tutorial Press, London.

Readers' Digest (1978), *The living world of animals*. Readers' Digest Association, London.

Tomkin, T.L.C. (1971), *Wild animals of the world in colour*. Blandford Press, Poole, Dorset.

Van den Brink, F.H. (1967), *A field guide to the mammals of Britain and Europe*. Collins, London.

Index of common names

Figures in **bold** *refer to colour plates. Other figures refer to text pages.*

aardvark 54, **20d**
addax 118, **29a**
agouti, golden 134, **36f**
anoa 124, **31d**
ant bear *see* aardvark
anteater
   Australian spiny *see* echidna
   banded *see* numbat, banded
   giant 51, **18e**
   marsupial *see* numbat, banded
   New Guinea 144–45, **43d**
   three-toed spiny *see* New Guinea
antelope
   harnessed *see* bushbuck
   roan 54, **20e**
   sable 53, **20b**
   saiga 48, **16e**
aoudad *see* Barbary sheep
argali 150, **45e**
armadillo
   Burmeister's fairy 51, **18d**
   giant 134, **36e**
   hairy 50–51, **18b**
ass, Persian wild *see* onager
aye aye 143, **42b**

babirusa 125, **31f**
baboon, yellow 53, **20a**
badger
   American 46–7, **15f**
   Eurasian 33, **10b**
   honey *see* ratel
bandicoot, rabbit 39–40, **13f**

banteng 124, **31c**
bat
   Australian fruit *see* fox, Australian flying
   pipistrelle 32–3, **10a**
   common vampire 132–3, **36a**
   greater Indian fruit 127, **33b**
bear
   ant *see* aardvark
   black 21–2, **6b**
   brown 24, **7d**
   grizzly 20, **5b**
   Malayan *see* sun
   polar 12, **1b**
   spectacled 151, **46b**
   sun 123–4, **31a**
beaver, Canadian 23, **6f**
bighorn *see* sheep, Rocky Mountain
bilby *see* bandicoot, rabbit
binturong 124, **31b**
bison, American 45–6, **15c**
blackbuck 49, **17d**
boar, wild 31, **9b**
bobcat *see* lynx, bay
buffalo
   African *see* Cape
   Cape 54–5, **20f**
   dwarf *see* anoa
   water 125, **31e**
bull, blue *see* nilgai
bushbaby, Senegal 140, **40c**
bushbuck 141, **40f**
bushpig 139–40, **40a**

camel
    Arabian 119, **29d**
    Bactrian 120, **30b**
capuchin
    black-capped *see* weeper
    weeper 133, **36b**
capybara 133, **36d**
caracal *see* lynx, Persian
caribou 15, **3b**
carpincho *see* capybara
cat
    golden 125–6, **32b**
    eastern native 39, **13a**
    European wild 32, **9e**
    sand-dune 119, **29e**
    spotted native 144, **43c**
chamois 150, **45c**
cheetah 50, **17f**
chevrotain
    Indian 126, **32d**
    water 140–41, **40e**
chimpanzee 140, **40d**
chinchilla 151, **46a**
chipmunk
    alpine 147–8, **44b**
    eastern 21, **5e**
civet
    African 140, **40b**
    common palm *see* musang
coati, white-nosed 133, **36c**
colugo 125, **32a**
cougar *see* puma
coyote 46, **15e**
cuscus, New Guinea spotted 144, **43b**

dassie *see* hyrax, rock
deer
    axis 126–7, **32f**
    barking *see* Chinese muntjac
    Chinese muntjac 38, **12e**
    Chinese water 37, **12d**
    chital *see* axis
    fallow 35–6, **11c**

mouse *see* chevrotain, Indian
    pampas 50, **18a**
    red 31–2, **9c**
    roe 33, **10c**
    sambar 126, **32e**
    white-tailed 29, **8d**
dik-dik, Kirk's 56, **21f**
dingo 39, **13d**
dog
    Azara's *see* fox, pampas
    Cape hunting 55–6, **21c**
    prairie *see* marmot, black-tailed prairie
dolphin, common 155, **48a**
dormouse, hazel 30–31, **9a**
dugong 156, **48c**
duiker
    Natal *see* red
    red 142, **41d**

echidna 112–13, **26e**
eland, common 56, **21e**
elephant
    African 55, **21e**
    Indian 128, **33d**
ermine *see* stoat
euro *see* wallaroo

fox
    Arctic 16, **4b**
    Australian flying 145, **43e**
    fennec 118–19, **29c**
    Indian flying 127, **33b**
    kit 116–17, **28a**
    pampas 52, **19b**
    red 34, **10f**

galidia 142–3, **42a**
gaur 128–9, **33f**
gazelle
    Dorcas 118, **29b**
    goitered 120, **30a**
    Grant's 56, **21d**
    Waller's *see* gerenuk

gerenuk 55, **21b**
gibbon
  lar 127, **33a**
  white-handed *see* lar
giraffe 57–8, **22d**
glider
  great 38, **13b**
  sugar 38, **13a**
glutton *see* wolverine
gnu, brindled *see* wildebeeste, blue
goat, Rocky Mountain 148, **44c**
gorilla 141, **41b**
grysbok 57, **22c**
guanaco 152, **46e**
guenon *see* monkey, vervet
guinea pig, pampas 53, **19e**

hamster, common 48, **16d**
here
  arctic *see* varying
  blue *see* varying
  brown 47, **16a**
  Patagonian *see* mara
  snowshoe *see* rabbit, snowshoe
  varying 17, **4d**
hartebeeste, bastard *see* sassaby
hedgehog
  European 33–4, **10d**
  long-eared 121, **30d**
hippopotamus 58, **22e**
hog
  giant forest 142, **41e**
  Red River *see* bushpig
  wart 110, **25a**
hyena, spotted 57, **22b**
hyrax, rock 58, **22f**

ibex
  alpine 150–51, **45f**
  Nubian 153, **47b**
impala 56–7, **22a**

jackal, black-backed 59, **23b**
jaguar 135, **37d**

jerboa, Egyptian 120–21, **30c**

kangaroo
  black tree 144, **43a**
  great grey 112, **26d**
  hill *see* wallaroo
  red 112, **26c**
kinkajou 134–5, **37b**
klipspringer 58, **23a**
koala 40, **14a**
kudu, greater 59, **23c**

langur, entellus 128, **33e**
lemming, Norwegian 17, **4c**
lemur
  flying *see* colugo
  ring-tailed 143, **42c**
leopard 127–8, **33c**
  clouded 129–30, **34d**
  snow 150, **45d**
linsang, spotted 130, **34e**
lion 60, **23g**
llama 152, **46d**
loris, slender 130, **34f**
lynx
  bay 29–30, **8e**
  Canadian 20, **5c**
  Persian 48–9, **17a**

mangabey, black 142, **41c**
mandrill 141, **41a**
mara 52, **19a**
marmoset
  black-tailed 135, **37e**
  golden lion 135, **37c**
marmot 20, **5d**
  alpine 149, **45a**
  black-tailed prairie 46, **15d**
  hoary 148–9, **44e**
marten
  American 21, **5f**
  pine 24, **7b**
meerkat, yellow *see* mongoose,
  yellow

mongoose
    Indian grey 49, **17c**
    ring-tailed *see* galidia
    slender 59, **23d**
    yellow 110, **24f**
monkey
    black spider *see* red-faced spider
    green *see* vervet
    Hanuman *see* langur, entellus
    red colobus 138, **39b**
    red howler 136, **37f**
    red-faced spider 134, **37a**
    rhesus 129, **34a**
    vervet 60, 109, **24a**
mole, European 34–5, **10g**
mole-rat 36, **11e**
moose 22, **6d**
mouflon 35, **11b**
mouse
    brush-tailed marsupial *see* phascogale, brush-tailed
    crest-tailed marsupial 112, **26b**
    hopping 114, **27f**
    kangaroo *see* hopping
    long-tailed field *see* wood
    pocket 118, **28e**
    wood 34, **10e**
musang 126, **32c**

nilgai 49–50, **17e**
numbat, banded 41, **14c**
nyala 109, **24d**

ocelot 137, **38d**
okapi 139, **39f**
onager 121, **30e**
opossum
    brush-tailed 40–41, **14b**
    common 28, **8a**
    Virginian *see* common
    woolly 136–7, **38c**
orangutan 129, **34b**
otter 32, **9f**

ounce *see* leopard, snow
ox
    musk 15, **3c**
    wood *see* anoa

paca 136, **38b**
pademelon, short-tailed *see* quokka
panda
    giant 37, **12b**
    red 36–7, **12a**
pangolin
    Cape 59–60, **23e**
    Indian 49, **17b**
    short-tailed *see* Cape
    small-scaled tree 139, **39d**
    Temminck's *see* Cape
panther, black *see* leopard
peccary, white-lipped 137, **38e**
phascogale, brush-tailed 41, **14d**
pichiciego, greater *see* armadillo, Burmeister's fairy
pig, earth *see* aardvark
platypus, duck-billed 42, **14f**
polecat, European 35, **11a**
porcupine
    African brush-tailed 138, **39c**
    Canadian 22, **6c**
    great crested 129, **34c**
    South African 60, **23f**
potaroo 113, **27a**
pronghorn 45, **15b**
puma 147, **44a**

quokka 111–12, **26a**
quoll *see* cat, eastern native

rabbit 36, **11d**
    black-tailed jack 117, **28c**
    snowshoe 22–3, **6e**
raccoon, North American 30, **8f**
rat
    black 31, **9d**
    desert wood 117, **28d**

long-nosed kangaroo *see* potaroo
Merriam's kangaroo 117, **28b**
moon 132, **35f**
ratel 54, **20c**
reedbuck 109–10, **24e**
rhinoceros
   black 109, **24b**
   Indian 132, **35e**

saiga *see* antelope, saiga
sassaby 109, **24c**
sea-lion, Californian 156–7, **48e**
seal
   crabeater 14, **2c**
   grey 157, **48f**
   Greenland *see* harp
   harp 13, **1d**
   ring 12, **1a**
   Ross 13, **2a**
   southern elephant 14, **2d**
   Weddell 13–14, **2b**
seladang *see* gaur
serval 111, **25e**
sheep
   Barbary 152, **47a**
   Dall's 148, **44d**
   Rocky Mountain 149, **44f**
   white *see* Dall's
shrew
   chequered elephant 139, **39e**
   common European 25, **7e**
skurk
   spotted 45, **15a**
   striped 30, **8g**
sloth, two-toed 137–8, **38f**
souslik
   Arctic 14–15, **3a**
   European 47–8, **16c**
springbok 120, **29f**
squirrel
   Arctic ground *see* souslik, Arctic
   grey 28–9, **8b**
   ground *see* souslik, European

five-striped palm 131, **35b**
North American flying 19, **5a**
red 23, **7a**
steinbok 111, **25c**
stoat 16, **4a**

tahr 37, **12c**
tamandua 136, **38a**
tapir, Malayan 130–31, **35a**
tarsier, Celebes 131, **35c**
Tasmanian devil 40, **13g**
tenrec 143, **42d**
thylacine *see* wolf, Tasmanian
tiger 131–32, **35d**
tucotuco 52–3, **19d**

unau *see* sloth, two-toed

vicuna 151–52, **46c**
viscacha, plains 52, **19c**
vole, water 47, **16b**
vontsira *see* galidia

wallaby
   brush *see* red-necked
   brush-tailed rock 113, **27c**
   hare 113, **27b**
   red-necked 114, **27e**
wallaroo 114, **27d**
walrus, Atlantic 13, **1c**
wapiti 29, **8c**
waterbuck, common 110, **25b**
weasel 25, **7f**
   least 21, **6a**
   short-tailed *see* stoat
whale
   Greenland right 156, **48d**
   sperm 155–6, **48b**
wildebeeste, blue 111, **25d**
wolf 15–16, **3d**
   maned 51, **18a**
   pouched *see* Tasmanian
   Tasmanian 41–2, **14e**

163

wolverine 24, **7c**
wombat 39, **13e**
woodchuck *see* marmot

yak, wild 149, **45b**

zebra, Cape mountain 153, **47c**

Index of Latin names

Figures in **bold** *refer to colour plates. Other figures refer to text pages.*

Acinonyx jubatus 50, **17f**
Addax nasomaculatus 118, **29a**
Aepyceros melampus 56–7, **22a**
Ailuropoda melanoleuca 37, **12b**
Ailurus fulgens 36–7, **12a**
Alces alces 22, **6d**
Alopex lagopus 16, **4b**
Alouatta seniculus 136, **37f**
Ammotragus lervia 152, **47a**
Anoa depressicornis 124, **31d**
Antidorcas marsupialis 120, **29f**
Antilocapra americana 45, **15b**
Antilope cervicapra 49, **17d**
Apodemus sylvaticus 34, **10e**
Arctictis binturong 124, **31b**
Arvicola terrestris 47, **16b**
Ateles paniscus 134, **37a**
Atherurus africanus 138, **39c**
Axis axis 126–7, **32f**

Babirussa babirussa 125, **31f**
Balaena mysticetus 156, **48d**
Bison bison 45–6, **15c**
Bos
   gaurus 128–9, **33f**
   javanicus 124, **31c**
   mutus 149, **45b**
Boselaphus tragocamelus 49–50, **17e**
Bubalus bubalis 125, **31e**
Burmeisteria retusa 51, **18d**

Callithrix melanura 135, **37e**
Caluromys lanatus 136–7, **38c**

Camelus
   bactrianus 120, **30b**
   dromedarius 119, **29d**
Canis
   dingo 39, **13d**
   latrans 46, **15e**
   lupus 15–16, **3d**
   mesomelas 59, **23b**
Capra
   ibex ibex 150–51, **45f**
   ibex nubiana 153, **47b**
Capreolus capreolus 33, **10c**
Castor canadensis 23, **6f**
Cavia pamparum 53, **19e**
Cebus nigrivittatus 133, **36b**
Cephalophus natalensis 142, **41d**
Cercocebus aterrimus 142, **41c**
Cercopithecus aethiops var. sabaeus 60, 109, **24a**
Cervus
   canadensis 29, **8c**
   elaphus 31–2, **9c**
   unicolor 126, **32e**
Chaetophractus villosus 50–51, **18b**
Chinchilla laniger 151, **46a**
Choloepus didactylus 137–8, **38f**
Chrysocyon brachyurus 51, **18c**
Citellus
   citellus 47–8, **16c**
   undulatus 14–15, **3a**
Colobus badius 138, **39b**
Connochaetes taurinus 111, **25d**
Cricetus cricetus 48, **16d**

165

Crocuta crocuta 57, **22b**
Ctenomys brasiliensis 52–3, **19d**
Cuniculus paca 136, **38b**
Cynictis penicillata 110, **24f**
Cynocephalus volans 125, **32a**
Cynomys ludovicianus 46, **15d**

Dama dama 35–6, **11c**
Damaliscus lunatus 109, **24c**
Dasyprocta aguti 134, **36f**
Dasyurops maculatus 144, **43c**
Dasyurus quoll 39, **13c**
Daubentonia madagascariensis 143, **42b**
Delphinus delphis 155, **48a**
Dendrolagus ursinus 144, **43a**
Desmodus rotundus 132–3, **36a**
Diceros bicornis 109, **24b**
Didelphis marsupialis 28, **8a**
Dipodomys merriami 117, **28b**
Dolichotis patagona 52, **19a**
Dugong dugon 156, **48c**
Dusicyon gymnocercus 52, **19b**

Echinosorex gymnurus 132, **35f**
Elephas maximus 128, **33d**
Equus
  hemionus onager 121, **30e**
  zebra 153, **47c**
Erethizon dorsatum 22, **6c**
Erinaceus europaeus 33–4, **10d**

Felis
  caracal 48–9, **17a**
  concolor 147, **44a**
  lynx canadensis 20, **5c**
  margarita 119, **29e**
  pardalis 137, **38d**
  rufa 29–30, **8e**
  serval 111, **25e**
  silvestris 32, **9e**
  temmincki 125–6, **32b**
Fennecus zerda 118–9, **29c**
Funambulus rufa 131, **35b**

Galago senegalensis 140, **40c**
Galidia elegans 142–3, **42a**
Gazella
  dorcas 118, **29b**
  granti 56, **21d**
  subgutturosa 120, **30a**
Giraffa camelopardalis 57–8, **22d**
Glaucomys volans 19, **5a**
Gorilla gorilla 141, **41b**
Gulo gulo 24, **7c**

Halichoerus grypus 157, **48f**
Helarctos malayanus 123–4, **31a**
Hemiechinus auritus 121, **30d**
Hemitragus jemlahicus 37, **12c**
Herpestes
  edwardsi 49, **17c**
  gracilis 59, **23d**
Hippopotamus amphibius 58, **22e**
Hippotragus
  equinus 54, **20e**
  niger niger 53, **20b**
Hydrochoerus hydrochaeris 133, **36d**
Hydropotes inermis 37, **12d**
Hyemoschus aquaticus 140–1, **40e**
Hylobates lar 127, **33a**
Hylochoerus meinertzhageni 142, **41e**
Hystrix
  africaeaustralis 60, **23f**
  cristata 129, **34c**

Jaculus jaculus 120–21, **30c**

Kobus ellipsiprymnus 110, **25b**

Lagorchestes leporoides 113, **27b**
Lagostomus maximus 52, **19c**
Lama
  glama 152, **46d**
  guanicoe 152, **46e**
Lemmus lemmus 17, **4c**
Lemur catta 143, **42c**
Leontideus rosalia 135, **37c**
Leptonychotes weddelli 13–14, **2b**

Lepus
  americanus 22–3, **6e**
  californicus 117, **28c**
  europaeus 47, **16a**
  timidus 17, **4d**
Litocranius walleri 55, **21b**
Lobodon carcinophagus 14, **2c**
Loris tardigradus 130, **34f**
Loxodonta africana 55, **21a**
Lutra lutra 32, **9f**
Lycaon pictus 55–6, **21c**

Macaca mulatta 129, **34a**
Macropus
  major 112, **26d**
  robustus 114, **27d**
  rufus 112, **26c**
Madoqua kirki 56, **21f**
Mandrillus sphinx 141, **41a**
Manis
  crassicaudata 49, **17b**
  temmincki 59–60, **23e**
  tricuspis 139, **39d**
Marmota
  caligata 148–9, **44e**
  marmota 149, **45a**
  monax 20, **5d**
Martes
  americana 21, **5f**
  mates 24, **7b**
Meles meles 33, **10b**
Mellivora capensis 54, **20c**
Mephitis mephitis 30, **8g**
Mirounga leonina 14, **2d**
Muntiacus reevesi 38, **12e**
Muscardinus avellanarius 30–1, **9a**
Mustela
  erminea erminea 16, **4a**
  nivalis nivalis 25, **7f**
  nivalis rixosa 21, **6a**
  putorius putorius 35, **11a**
Myrmecobius fasciatus 41, **14c**
Myrmecophaga tridactyla 51, **18e**

Nasua narica 133, **36c**
Neofelis nebulosa 129–30, **34d**
Neotoma lepida 117, **28d**
Notomys mitchelli 114, **27f**

Odobenus rosmarus rosmarus 13, **1c**
Odocoileus virginianus 29, **8d**
Okapia johnstoni 139, **39f**
Ommatophoca rossi 13, **2a**
Oreamnos americanus 148, **44c**
Oreotragus oreotragus 58, **23a**
Ornithorhynchus anatinvs 42, **14f**
Orycteropus afer 54, **20d**
Oryctolagus cuniculus 36, **11d**
Ovibos moschatus 15, **3c**
Ovis
  ammon 150–1, **45f**
  canadensis 149, **44f**
  dalli 148, **44d**
  musimon 35, **11b**
Ozotoceras bezoarticus 50, **18a**

Pagophilus groenlandicus 13, **1d**
Pan troglodytes 140, **40d**
Panthera
  leo 60, **23g**
  onca 135, **37d**
  pardus 127–8, **33c**
  tigris 131–2, **35d**
  uncia 150, **45d**
Papio cynocephalus 53, **20a**
Paradoxurus hermaphroditus 126, **32c**
Perodicticus potto 138, **39a**
Perognathus penicillatus 118, **28e**
Petaurus sciureus 38, **13a**
Petrogale penicillata 113, **27c**
Phacochoerus aethiopicus 110, **25a**
Phalanger maculatus 144, **43b**
Phascogale tapoatafa 41, **14d**
Phascolarctos cinereus 40, **14a**
Physeter catodon 155–6, **48b**
Pipistrellus pipistrellus 32–3, **10a**
Pongo pygmaeus 129, **34b**
Potamochoerus porcus 139–40, **40a**

Potorous tridactylus 113, **27a**
Potus flavus 134–5, **37b**
Presbytis entellus 128, **33e**
Priodontes giganteus 134, **36e**
Prionodon pardicolor 130, **34c**
Procavia capensis capensis 58, **22f**
Procyon lotor 30, **8f**
Pteropus
   giganteus 127, **33b**
   poliocephalus 145, **43e**
Pusa hispida 12, **1a**

Rangifer tarandus caribou 15, **3b**
Raphicerus
   campestris 111, **25c**
   melanotis 57, **22c**
Rattus rattus 31, **9d**
Redunca arundinum 109–110, **24e**
Rhinoceros unicornis 132, **35e**
Rhynchocyon cirnei 139, **39e**
Rupicapra rupicapra 150, **45c**

Saiga tatarica 48, **16e**
Sarcophilus harrisii 40, **13g**
Schoinobates volans 38, **13b**
Sciurus
   carolinensis 28–9, **8b**
   vulgaris 23, **7a**
Setonix brachyurus 111–12, **26a**
Sminthopsis crassicaudata 112, **26b**
Sorex araneus 25, **7e**
Spalax microphthalamus 36, **11e**
Spilogale putorius 45, **15a**
Sus scrofa 31, **9b**
Syncerus caffer 54–5, **20f**

Tachyglossus aculeatus 112–13, **26e**
Talpa europaea 34–5, **10g**

Tamandua tetradactyla 136, **38a**
Tamias
   alpinus 147–8, **44b**
   striatus 21, **5e**
Tapirus indicus 130–31, **35a**
Tarsius spectrum 131, **35c**
Taurotragus oryx oryx 56, **21e**
Taxidea taxus 46–7, **15f**
Tayassu albirostris 137, **38e**
Tenrec ecaudatus 143, **42d**
Thalarctos maritimus 12, **1b**
Thylacinus cynocephalus 41–2, **14e**
Thylacomys lagotis 39–40, **13f**
Tragelaphus
   angasi 109, **24d**
   scriptus 141, **40f**
   strepsiceros 59, **23c**
Tragulus meminna 126, **32d**
Tremarctos ornatus 151, **46b**
Trichosurus vulpecula 40–41, **14b**

Ursus
   americanus 21–22, **6b**
   arctos 24, **7d**
   arctos horribilis 20, **5b**

Vicugna vicugna 151–2, **46c**
Viverra civetta 140, **40b**
Vombatus ursinus 39, **13e**
Vulpes
   velox 116–17, **28a**
   vulpes vulpes 34, **10f**

Wallabia rufogrisea 114, **27e**

Zaglossus bruijni 144–5, **43d**
Zalophus californianus 156–7, **48e**